FOOL A CARNIVORE

MEATY MAIN DISHES...MINUS THE MEAT

NANCY OLAH

ISBN: 0615636608
ISBN-13: 9780615636603

Library of Congress Control Number: 2012938577
CreateSpace, North Charleston, SC

Imprint: Fool Carnivores, LLC

DEDICATION

This book is dedicated to the two carnivores in my family:

- My wonderful husband, Bill Pace, who despite being a carnivore, has been willing and eager to eat everything I've cooked since we met in 1981, and who has faithfully cleaned up after this very messy cook; and
- Our handsome son, Nick Pace, who I tried to raise as a vegetarian, but who chose the "dark side" in his teens. Despite his new found love of meat, Nick has eaten every dish I've created and has been my most ardent supporter in this project.

I could not have written this book without the constant love, faith, and support of the two fabulous men in my life.

Figure 1 - Nancy and her two favorite carnivores

TABLE OF CONTENTS

SPICY SAUSAGE DISHES (CHORIZO OR CHIPOTLE SAUSAGE)

BRATWURST AND KIELBASA

SMOKED APPLE SAGE SAUSAGE

ACKNOWLEDGEMENTS

In addition to my husband, Bill Pace, and our son, Nick Pace, to whom this book is dedicated, I want to thank the other people who have helped and encouraged me through this long process.

The first person I want to thank is Deborah Madison, one of my culinary heroes. Deborah took the time to read my manuscript and offer me constructive, wise, and incisive suggestions on how to improve my recipes. Deborah was kind enough to respond to my initial email to her website, and entered into an email dialogue with me. She agreed to meet with me at her peaceful home in New Mexico and gently helped me see all the silly, novice mistakes I had made in my manuscript. Her encouraging emails have been one of the highlights of the past few months as I remade all my recipes, taking more care in noting timing and measurements. I have admired Deborah as an author and chef for over twenty-five years. The gift of her time and experience in helping this fledgling author get this book out of its nest was a gracious act of generosity and kindness.

Figure 2. I was honored to receive Deborah Madison's helpful feedback on my book

My friend Shannon Nash became a vegetarian during the past year and dropped forty-five pounds as she began to test many of my recipes. I loved to hear Shannon's reports of how she fooled her teenage carnivore son, Justin, who wolfed down the food she prepared from my recipes.

My friend Gina Elliott researched self-publishing options, helped me with my website and Facebook page, and provided me with creative feedback about how to market my book.

My friend Anne Willkomm spent many hours reading my manuscript and offering constructive editing advice. Anne also introduced me to one of her former students, the multi-talented Jenny Ford, who prepared the index and offered helpful suggestions about the cover.

Many other friends and colleagues gave me support and encouragement at various points during this process: Patty Frost-Brooks, Patti Tracey, Chris Hudson, Geoff Gray, Angie Dugick, Dawn Royle, Carrie Sharp, Mary Ann Rouse, Jeanne LaBelle, Brenda Dohring Hicks, Georgette Vidmar, Vivian Santiago, Gladys Howard, Cindy Speas Moore, Don Johns, Cindy Wolfe, Emily Scofield, Steve Kaplan, Ellen Linares, Karen Bennetts, Nancia and Giancarlo Dalimonte, Amy Clement, Sarah Funkhouser, Dawn Becker, Kathryn Haidet, Liz Schroeder, Denise and Mark Schnitzer, Caroline Webber, Melanie Connellee, Rachel Cogar, Nancy Himes, Lisa Jobs, Paul Burton, Deb Pero, Beth Chuck, Jeanie and Fred Taylor, Diane LaPoint, Debbie Risko Muccio, Ray and Elizabeth Conforti, Karen Clapperton, Brenda Kluttz, Woody Farmer, Marion Tevebaugh, Lora Nichols, Dan Ballou, Carol Connor, Anthony Pitrella, Sarah Shifflet, Sheila Neisler, Cathy Harris, Caroline Prochnau, and Linda Turner. My mom, Ida Olah, and my mother-in-law, Margaret Pace, were always there for me whenever I needed a boost.

Last, but not least, I'd like to thank the folks at CreateSpace for helping me to realize my vision.

INTRODUCTION

As a product of the North, I grew up with "potluck" suppers. As a resident of the South since 1981, I quickly learned the more genteel custom of "covered dish" dinners.

In December 2010, I brought a beautiful baking dish of homemade lasagna to a covered dish dinner to celebrate the holidays with a group of people who didn't know me very well. I positioned my lasagna on a trivet, uncovered it, and went into the kitchen to socialize over a glass of wine.

About twenty minutes later, my husband hurried into the kitchen and whispered to me that if I wanted to have anything to eat, I better get into the dining room quickly. Even though there were platters of ham and chicken (along with the obligatory sausage balls), everyone had gravitated toward my lasagna. There were only two or three pieces left, out of a very large pan. I helped myself to a piece, added salad to my plate, and was glad that my husband had alerted me to the dwindling supply of the one vegetarian main dish on the table.

After desert, many people came up and complimented me on my lasagna. Several asked if I would share my recipe with them. I quickly realized that none of them knew that the lasagna hadn't contained meat. It looked and smelled like meat, and had a great taste (thanks to my homemade sauce, fresh herbs from my garden, and excellent fresh mozzarella). When I finally admitted that it was meatless lasagna, made with one of the vegetarian meat analogues I'll recommend in this book, people were stunned. Several men in the group who professed to "hate vegetarian food" had taken large helpings and had cleaned their plates.

That evening motivated me to get serious about a project I had been working on for several years. My goal was to create a cookbook for vegetarians who live in families of carnivores and who are trying to keep the peace, along with their sanity. Instead of cooking separate meals for themselves and meat for their families, what if I could show them how to fix meals that would satisfy their carnivorous spouse or offspring, and fool them into thinking they were eating the dish they expected?

I've based this cookbook on how to take familiar, classic meat recipes and adapt them to the growing array of vegetarian products in our stores. When I became a vegetarian in 1974, there were very few meat analogues. I ate a lot of brown rice, stir-fries, tofu, tempeh, seitan, salads, and pasta. I made my own yogurt, whole grain bread, and tofu since it was hard to find these products in conventional grocery stores. When I tried to talk with people about why I became a vegetarian, I watched their eyes glaze over as they imagined their plates minus the meat.

In 1981, I met a wonderful Southern man and total carnivore who enjoyed good food. Bill was open to eating anything I cooked, and within a year, had effortlessly shed twenty pounds, while noticeably improving his health and energy levels. We married in 1983 and were blessed with our son, Nick, in 1993. Although Nick occasionally ate chicken nuggets at the homes of his friends, he was basically a vegetarian until a Boy Scout camping trip in 2004. Nick got into camp late the first night. All the cheese pizza had been eaten, so Nick went to bed hungry. In the morning, he woke to the tantalizing smell of bacon. His fellow Scouts, knowing he was a vegetarian, left a rasher of bacon in front of his tent. One bite was all it took to make him wonder why his mom, who professed to love him, would have withheld the wondrous taste of bacon from him all those years!

When Nick returned from camp, he began to eat more meat at friends' homes and at restaurants. I decided that I needed to find some ways to make my cooking more appealing to him. I began experimenting with each new vegetarian meat analogue that came on the market and learned how to adapt them to conventional meat recipes, with ever greater success.

This cookbook has been almost seven years in the making. I want you to learn from my mistakes. You can't simply substitute meat analogues in a conventional recipe and expect them to behave in the same way as meat. Cooking methods, times, and sequencing are not the same as in a standard meat recipe. Products can also vary dramatically in taste and texture. I may recommend a specific product for one recipe, but a completely different product for another application. I've tried all of them, multiple times, on a trial-and-error basis. I hope you can benefit from my many mistakes by following my recipes to get the best results. Please check out my website at www.foolacarnivore.com for color photos of my recipes, helpful hints, and a new recipe every week.

The title of my book is meant in a playful way. If something looks and tastes like meat, and is healthier and lower in fat and calories, what's wrong with passing it off as meat? If you are a vegetarian in a family of carnivores, then stop fighting and start fooling. Try my recipes, keep your mouth shut, and be grateful when your family compliments you on a delicious meal. Go ahead, wink behind their backs, and fool a carnivore!

Is This Book For You?

This book is aimed at the following people:

- Vegetarians who live in a family of carnivores and who are either making two different dinners every night or are making themselves or their families unhappy.

- People who want to become vegetarians, but are concerned about getting enough protein or just can't get used to the sight of their plates minus the meat.

- Carnivores who have a child or spouse who wants to become a vegetarian.

- Flexitarians–people who do not want to become vegetarians, but who want their families to eat healthier (the Meatless Monday crowd).

MY CULINARY HEROES

I want to acknowledge and thank the chefs and cookbook authors who have guided and influenced me in my life's journey as a cook. Like many people from my generation, I started with *Betty Crocker's Cook Book for Boys and Girls* at the age of eight. My very tattered copy is evidence that I cooked the tar out of those simple recipes. However, many of them used pre-made mixes, so I quickly outgrew this book and was hungry for a new challenge.

I found that challenge when a local Cleveland TV station began broadcasting Julia Child's "The French Chef." I glued myself to our black-and-white TV set every week and took copious notes. Since I didn't yet have her cookbook, I was determined to surprise my parents by making her dishes at Sunday dinner. For those of you thinking, "What does this vegetarian know about making meat dishes?" I can testify that I learned from Julia how to make coq au vin, cassoulet, steak au poivre, rognons sautés et flambés, boeuf bourguignon, French onion soup, and pistou, along with a killer hollandaise sauce, all before the age of ten. When I finally got a paperback edition of her book, *The French Chef*, for my birthday, I literally wore it out from loving it too much!

I gradually realized that butter, eggs, dairy, and meat—luscious though they might be—were not the best fuel for a healthy body. By my mid-teens, Adele Davis entered my life with a trio of books, *Let's Cook it Right*, *Let's Have Healthy Children*, and *Let's Eat Right to Keep Fit*. Just as I had with Julia, I threw myself into the mode of healthier cooking. Mind you, I was still cooking and eating meat. My battered copy of *Let's Cook it Right* shows liver and onions, liver baked with wine, and kidneys flaming with brandy all dutifully checked off to show I made them (although it's hard for me to imagine today).

By eighteen, I began to have qualms about consuming so much meat. I read *Diet for a Small Planet* by Frances Moore Lappé, and was totally sold on her passionate treatise that explained why Americans should reduce our meat consumption if we truly care about feeding everyone on our planet. Lappé described how the modern agri-business practice of feeding grain and soy to livestock means that cows are actually protein factories in reverse.[1] The revelation that it took sixteen pounds of grain and soy to produce one pound of beef made me very militant. I remember having horrible arguments with my father at restaurants like the Brown Derby, when he insisted that I order a steak and I then refused to eat it. Unfortunately, my dad died when I was nineteen. His untimely death at the age of forty-seven shook me up. As a junior at Oberlin College, it was easy for me to move into full-blown vegetarian mode, since there were always non-meat alternatives at a hippie school like Oberlin. These were the days when *The Vegetarian Epicure* by Anna Thomas became my culinary bible.

In 1977, as a student at University of Michigan Law School, I discovered Mollie Katzen's *Moosewood Cookbook*, and cooked every recipe in the tiny kitchen of my off-campus apartment. I volunteered at a local food co-op, putting in my time each week to "earn" a loaf of bread or a pound of tofu, along with a precious ten percent discount on groceries and produce.

---

1   Frances Moore Lappé, *Diet for a Small Planet* (New York: Ballantine Books, 1973), 4.

Returning to Cleveland in 1978 as a young attorney at a large law firm, I was no longer in a safe hippie environment like Oberlin or Ann Arbor, where being a vegetarian was accepted and understood. Without food co-ops or a decent health food store, I had to bake my own bread, culture my own yogurt, and make my own soy milk and tofu. I moved to Charlotte, North Carolina in 1981 and experienced an even bigger culture shock because the South was not friendly to vegetarians in that era. Fortunately, I soon met my future husband and we were married two years later. Although Bill is a carnivore, he loves good food and home-cooked meals, and proved to be receptive to my vegetarian cooking.

In 1987, on a trip to San Francisco, Bill and I ate at the legendary restaurant Greens. I purchased Deborah Madison's *The Greens Cook Book*, and felt like I had discovered a kindred spirit. Deborah quickly became one of my favorite authors with *The Savory Way*, *This Can't be Tofu!*, *Vegetarian Cooking for Everyone*, and *Local Flavors*, providing guidance and inspiration in my kitchen over many years.

Other culinary influences include *Simple and Healthy Cooking* by Jacques Pépin; *In Pursuit of Flavor* by Edna Lewis; *Greene on Greens* by Bert Greene; *The Passionate Vegetarian* by Crescent Dragonwagon; *Cook with Jamie* by Jamie Oliver; *Patricia Wells' Trattoria* by Patricia Wells; *The Classic Pasta Cookbook* by Giuliano Hazan; and every book Marcella Hazan has written, but especially *Essentials of Classic Italian Cooking* and *Marcella Cucina*.

I am not a formally trained chef. I have not been to culinary school and I have never cooked in a restaurant kitchen. I learned how to cook simply by cooking almost every day since I was a kid. These are my culinary heroes: the women and men who have taught, influenced, and inspired me. Each of them has helped to make me a better cook, and I owe them a huge debt of gratitude.

Figure 3. I was thrilled to meet Jacques Pépin and watch him cook at the 13th *Annual Food & Wine Magazine Classic at Aspen* (June 1995)

Figure 4. I learned so much watching Guiliano Hazan make pasta at the 13th *Annual Food & Wine Magazine Classic at Aspen* (June 1995)

Figure 5. I fulfilled a lifelong dream when I met Julia Child at the 13th *Annual Food & Wine Magazine Classic at Aspen* (June 1995)

Figure 6. The incomparable Julia in action making salade Niçoise at the 13th *Annual Food & Wine Magazine Classic at Aspen* (June 1995)

BELIEVE IN THE VALUE OF FAMILY MEALS

One of the reasons I committed the time to write this book is that I believe in the value of families sitting down together to enjoy a home-cooked family meal. We all lead such busy lives. It is easy for families to get pulled in different directions with work, social commitments, after-school practices and activities, civic responsibilities, and non-profit events. I have many friends whose families literally eat on the run between activities, or eat on a "serial basis," with people coming and going at different times. I am a busy attorney with volunteer leadership roles on several non-profit boards and have been a working mother throughout my son's life. However, we have home-cooked family meals at least five nights per week. I think that taking the easy escape of ordering take-out or defrosting a frozen pizza can shortchange and trivialize the experience of a family dinner. The process of cooking a healthy dinner for my husband and son, and then eating together while we talk gives me a feeling of satisfaction and accomplishment that my "paid job" doesn't provide.

Our son tells me how few of his friends actually have family mealtimes. Based on 2010 information from the United States Department of Labor, Bureau of Labor Statistics, the entire civilian population over the age of fifteen spends 0.56 hours per day on meal preparation and cleanup, and spends 2.7 hours per day watching television. Breaking down this data further by sex, 41.3 percent of men and 67.5 percent of women reported engaging in daily food preparation or cleanup, with men spending 0.77 hours per day and women spending an average of 1.16 hours per day.[2]

In a digital world where we increasingly communicate in a variety of non-personal ways, the only way to really know what's going on in the lives of our family members is by talking face-to-face and spending quality time together. I think that one of the biggest reasons our family weathered the stormy teen years so well is that we talked with our son Nick over dinner almost every day.

While I realize that not everyone has time every evening for a sit down family meal, I have tried hard to make that happen for my family. In the process, I have discovered that the following tips make for a more enjoyable experience and improve the quality of our family meal time:

- Even if you are tired and tempted to use paper plates and napkins, please consider setting the table with a tablecloth or placemats, cloth napkins, and proper dishes, glasses, and cutlery. Admit that you have a different attitude toward food served in a nice restaurant as opposed to a burger you bought at a fast food joint. You and your family will appreciate the effort you're making to cook them a meal from scratch if you or a family member spends the three minutes it takes to properly set your table. If you have kids, setting the table is an ideal job for them. Our son started setting the table when he was about four years old. Since he could count and was learning to spell, here's how I taught him where things go. The word "left" has four letters, and so does the word "fork," so they always go to the left of the plate, with the salad fork on the outside, and the dinner fork right next to the plate. The word "right" has five letters, and so do the words "knife," "spoon," and "glass," so they always go the right of the plate. The knife goes first, with the blade edge toward the plate with

---

2   United States Department of Labor, Bureau of Labor Statistics, http://www.bls.gov/news.release/atus.t01.htm

the spoon next to it, and the glass above the two utensils, in the two o'clock position in relation to the plate. The napkin either goes to the left, next to the salad fork, or in the center of the plate. You probably know this already, but I've been surprised at the number of adults I meet who honestly don't know how to set the table. Please try it and you might be surprised at the difference it makes in your family's attitude and appreciation of the effort you've spent cooking them a delicious meal.

- Turn the television off, and turn on some beautiful background music.

- Hold hands and connect with each other while saying grace. Never eat a meal without giving thanks for the food you are about to eat.

- Let the phone go to voicemail while you're having dinner.

- No texting at the table.

- Don't just talk about your day at work or at school—talk about what's going on in the world or your hopes, dreams, and aspirations. Conversation needs to be more than just a litany of problems at your job, complaints about teachers or coaches, money woes, negative diatribes, or destructive comments. I'd be lying if I claimed we have never had disagreements or arguments during a family meal. We have had our share. However, festering problems or issues we avoided discussing might have stayed submerged and unresolved if we hadn't taken the time to talk about them.

- Unless someone has an important commitment, no one should be excused from the table until everyone is done eating.

- The rule in our home is whoever has cooked dinner does not have to clean up. If I've spent time planning and cooking a delicious meal, the family members who enjoyed it should wash the dishes and clean the kitchen. Doesn't that seem fair?

How To Use This Book

Please follow these few easy tips to get the most out of this book.

- **Follow Directions** — Recipe steps are listed in a certain order for a reason. Meat analogues cook differently than meat, so you can't simply use them in your favorite meat recipe without making appropriate modifications. I've developed and tested all these recipes, and have tried many different variations of each recipe. I've also enlisted a select group of friends who have been my testers. The ones I've given you in this book have given us good results, so please try to follow each recipe as closely as you can.

- **Don't Make Substitutions in the Meat Analogues** — It's tempting to want to make substitutions, especially if a different brand of meat analogue is on sale. (Hey, aren't all vegetarian sausage products the same?) Unfortunately, they are *not* all the same. There are significant differences in texture and taste among meat analogues. Different products work better for certain recipes than others. If I recommend a specific brand of meat analogue chicken cutlet, for example, I sought out and tried every brand of that product I could find before I made the recommendation. Please review the section entitled "Meat Analogues" in which I describe the various products used in this cookbook and provide information from the websites of the companies that make those products. Substitute if you must, but please trust my suggestions in specific recipes for the best results.

- **Feel Free to Make Other Substitutions That Suit Your Family's Palate** — Since I just advised you not to make substitutions in the meat analogues, you may wonder why I am giving you free rein to make other recipe substitutions. The reason is that the whole point of these recipes is to find ways to fool your family carnivores. You know better than anyone what they like to eat, and how spicy or bland they may like their food. For example, if you know they hate garlic, the four cloves of garlic I use in my Bolognese sauce may turn them off. Or if they love spicy foods, you're going to want to add lots of jalapeños to the Mexican Pizza. If someone in your family is allergic to nuts or has an aversion to a certain vegetable, make appropriate substitutions. If a family member can't eat soy or is gluten intolerant, you'll want to check the section on meat analogues to see what products to safely substitute.

- **If You Have a Choice, Choose Organic** — In my section entitled "Other Ingredients," I've made many specific recommendations of organic products (for example, Muir Glen Diced Tomatoes). I've done that because I think it is a vastly superior product and will give you better results than a can of conventionally grown diced tomatoes. In other places, my ingredient list may just say "green beans" or "carrots." I've deliberately done that because I recognize that many of you may not have access to good quality organic produce at a reasonable cost. My approach is to always buy organic produce if it is available unless the price differential between it and conventionally grown produce is a lot more than I am willing to pay. However, if the cost difference is nominal, I always choose organic. I personally don't like the idea of using petroleum-based chemicals, synthetic fertilizers, and harmful pesticides on the fruits and vegetables I eat. I also don't like the use of a nonrenewable energy source to produce these chemicals, since what isn't absorbed by the plants goes into our storm water systems, and ultimately our waterways. I don't want to drink milk or eat cheese or yogurt made from farm animals that are fed antibiotics or synthetic growth hormones. Last, but not least, the more I learn about genetically engineered crops (commonly called GMOs), the more concerned I've become.[3] Since the Food and Drug Administration does not require that labels indicate if ingredients come from GMO sources, the only way I can tell if a product does not contain GMOs is if the manufacturer voluntarily states that it uses non-GMO sources or if the product has a USDA Organic label. I think organic food tastes better, has greater nutritional benefits, and is a safer alternative than conventionally grown food. If your pocketbook permits and it's available, I urge you to consider choosing organic whenever possible.

- **If You Have a Choice, Choose Locally Grown Produce** — I grew up eating local produce, with very little purchased from the grocery store during the peak summer months. I had a school garden from third grade until my senior year of high school that produced enough vegetables to feed our family. My mom grew strawberries and raspberries in our backyard in Cleveland, and my grandpa grew tomatoes, eggplant, zucchini, and peppers. I felt blessed to have such an abundance of fresh vegetables and fruit that I could use in my cooking. Now I call the Carolinas my home. I live in Fort Mill, South Carolina, and work in Charlotte, North Carolina. I feel fortunate to have a wonderful regional farmers' market in Charlotte about fifteen miles from my home. To me, a farmers' market is about value, freshness, and quality. Your local farmers' market is probably a good source for organic produce (or at least local produce grown without pesticides and herbicides). Talk with the farmers. Often, the strict rules around organic labeling don't allow farmers to advertise that they are organic because their fields aren't certified or they haven't been in business for the required length of time. We also grow some of our own vegetables and all of our herbs in our backyard. We recently purchased a "share" in a Community Supported Agriculture (CSA) program that gives us locally grown produce from June to early September. When you are buying and eating locally grown produce, you are eating with the seasons, and your diet will be more balanced and varied throughout the year. A good place to learn more about CSA programs and to locate one in your area is http://www.localharvest.org.

Figure 7. The bounty from my school vegetable garden–circa 1964

---

3   The best film I've seen about GMOs is *The Future of Food*, a compelling documentary by Deborah Koons Garcia. Before you decide how you feel about GMOs, please seek out the film and watch it with an open mind. For more information check out http://www.thefutureoffood.com.

- **Be Flexible in Your Approach to Meals to Take Advantage of Bargains** – For those of you who plan your week's meals in advance, don't be afraid to deviate from recipes or stock up when certain products are on sale. As a working mother, I understand the need to stretch the dollars in your food budget and am a big advocate of using coupons on pantry staples. However, when I go to the farmers' market, I'm very flexible and unstructured. I rarely set out with a shopping list or a specific menu in mind. I am guided by what's freshest, and then build my meals around those ingredients. I also frequently find wonderful bargains at the market. I picked up a lovely bunch of local organic golden beets for $1, and the week before bought three large bunches of Asian long beans for $5 (normally, $3 per bunch). Today, a local farmer had gorgeous asparagus that was just picked yesterday. I tend to shop the market around noon when the sellers are interested in going home and are eager to unload any produce that didn't sell in the morning. Your selection may be more limited, but you can often get excellent quality for a fraction of the price that the early morning shoppers paid.

- **Recipe Categories** – I've broken down my recipes into five sections:

  - **Ground Meat**
  - **Sausage**
  - **Beef**
  - **Chicken**
  - **Bacon**

  I've further broken them down into three very basic types of recipes:

  - **Easy Weeknight Meals** (recipes that can be made in thirty minutes or less)
  - **Slow Cooker** (recipes you can assemble in the slow cooker before you leave for work)
  - **Weekend Dinners** (more complicated recipes which will take you an hour or more to prepare–but are well worth the extra time)

  I thought long and hard about including a separate section of "Sides"—that flexible Southern term for anything that is not the main dish—except dessert! I decided that the focus of this cookbook needed to be on my meatless main dishes. Although I have made suggestions of appropriate side dishes in many recipes, I have only included recipes for sides if I thought that they really added something essential to the main dish. Please stay tuned for my next book that will include a whole section of delectable sides to accompany more of my meaty meatless main dishes.

- **Focus on Your Cooking** – This may seem like a silly or obvious suggestion, but since it's a rule I often ignore myself (to the detriment of my dish), I thought I'd include it. There have been way too many times when I've burned the garlic, or overcooked the pasta because I thought I could throw in a load of clothes, check my email, or return a phone call while I was cooking. All of us like to think we're better at multi-tasking than we actually are. What I've found is that when I try to do other things while also getting our dinner on the table, it actually takes me longer, and my results are not as good. "Thirty-minute meals" means that you need to give the tasks before you a solid thirty minutes of your attention. If you're not experienced in the kitchen, you probably should add another ten minutes to the equation because some of the prep work may take you longer until you gain experience. On the other hand, if you can enlist the help of your spouse or kids, you may be able to shave off ten minutes, because many things can be done at the same time.

- **Accept Help in the Kitchen** – There's an old saying that "many hands make light work." It comes from an era when people worked together to tackle a big task, got it done more quickly, and enjoyed each other's company during the process. The biggest challenge for me in accepting help in the kitchen is letting go of my quest for perfection. For example, the vegetables may not be cut as perfectly or as evenly as I would do them, but they will still taste good in the finished dish. My advice is to read through a recipe completely and figure out what tasks you can easily delegate, and what things you trust only yourself to handle. When my son was home on spring break from college, we worked together, side-by-side, on one of my "Weekend Dinner" recipes. Not only did we shorten the prep time dramatically, it also provided a relaxed, informal setting for him to share some of the things that were going on with classes, friends and roommates that he might not have otherwise told me. Afterwards, when we were eating dinner, he told me how much he enjoyed the time we spent preparing the delicious meal together.

- **Cooking Requires Non-Linear Thinking** – Becoming a good cook requires some non-linear thinking. Non-linear thinking is creative thought and doesn't flow in a straight line from one point to the next. One of the challenges of translating what I do to create a meal into words is that cooking often doesn't lend itself to precise step-by- step instructions. Consequently, I use the time while the onions are cooking, the sauce is simmering, or the pot of water for pasta is heating, to grate the cheese, make the salad, or prep the other vegetables. I find it hard to explain that process using a precise sequence in written recipes. By having a clear goal (getting a healthy meal on the table for your family in a reasonable amount of time) and focusing only on what you need to do to reach that goal, you may find that cooking is a lot more fun, creative, and satisfying than you ever thought possible. Please check out my website (http://www.foolacarnivore.com) for links to my cooking videos that will help you learn how to sharpen your non-linear thinking skills to make the most of your time in the kitchen.

- **Cook with a Glad Heart** – If you approach the preparation of meals as drudgery, rather than an act of love for your family, you will not enjoy cooking. I believe that everything you do should be done with a "glad heart." There are many biblical references to having a cheerful heart or a glad heart, and to me it all boils down to your attitude. I feel that I'm serving both God and my family by making the preparation of a healthy dinner a daily priority. Before our son left for college, he often went to school with a skimpy breakfast or none at all. I made a healthy lunch for him, but knew his lunch box would often have half-eaten food in it when he returned home. His dinner was the one meal of the day that I could control, and that was because we all ate together as a family. No matter how challenging my day was at work, I tried to set aside that strife when I returned home, so that I could focus on cooking a delicious healthy meal for my family. Even if you are not a person of faith, my bet is that you love your family and want what's best for them. So, if you love your family and believe that good health depends on the nourishment we give our bodies, doesn't it make sense to cook with a glad heart?

- **Meat Analogues are Not Immune from Spoilage** – We have all seen news articles about the increasing number of people who get food poisoning every year by eating improperly prepared, stored, or cooked meat or poultry. The Mayo Clinic website describes the many different contaminants that cause food-borne illness, such as E. coli, campylobacter, salmonella, clostridium perfingens, and listeria.[4] However, meat analogues that have not been properly stored or prepared can also become

---

4   Mayo Clinic Staff, MayoClinic.com, Mayo Foundation, June 18, 2011, accessed March 15, 2012. http://www.mayoclinic.com/health/food-poisoning/DS00981/DSECTION=causes

spoiled and can make you ill. Pay attention to the "best used by" dates on the packages. If you don't think you will use it by that date, store it in the freezer (and remember when you put it there). If you only use a portion of a product, refrigerate it promptly in an air tight bag or container. If you open that container a few days later and the meat analogue has a slimy texture, smells funny, or has any mold on it, you need to throw it out. Please use common sense. Although I hate to waste food, it is not worth getting sick because you couldn't bear to throw two sausages away. If you decide you want to freeze the meat analogue, check the package or the company's website to see the recommendations for the length of time it can be safely stored in the freezer. Always check for freezer burn which may affect the texture and taste of the product. Again, when in doubt, just throw it out.

- **Start with Sausage First** – My sausage recipes are the ones most readily embraced by meat-eaters, because many of the products on the market really duplicate the look, taste, and texture of meat. My suggestion is to pick a dish that is familiar to your family–or a particular sausage that they really enjoy–and start there.

Good luck feeding your family carnivores!

MEAT ANALOGUES

I've called this section "Meat Analogues," instead of "Meat Substitutes," "Pretend Meat," "Faux Meat," or "Fake Meat," all of which have negative connotations. To me, an analogue is something that is similar or analogous to something else, but is different in structure, origin, or content. These products are standing in for the meat in a conventional recipe, but instead of looking at what you're missing without the meat, look instead at the benefits of using a meat analogue instead of the real deal. Most of the meat analogues have the following characteristics:

- Lower in fat, particularly saturated fat
- Lower in calories
- Zero cholesterol
- High in protein
- More fiber
- High in sodium (their one major drawback)[5]

I was struck by how quickly the media picked up the results of a study called "Red Meat Consumption and Mortality," which recently appeared in the online edition of the Archives of Internal Medicine.[6] This twenty-year study involved the health and eating habits of over 110,000 adults. It concluded that all red meat is bad for you and that even a daily three-ounce serving of unprocessed red meat increased the risk of dying during the study by 13 percent. Even worse, a daily serving of a processed red meat, such as hot dogs, sausage, or bacon was associated with a 20 percent greater risk of dying during the study. Most of the people in the study ate at least one serving of red meat per day, so imagine the risk we run— and perhaps even more important, our nation's children run—by eating several meat-based meals each day. The researchers also validated what I've believed for many years: replacing meat with healthier sources of protein, such as nuts, whole grains, low-fat dairy, and legumes can reduce your mortality risk.

One of the reasons I became a vegetarian at the age of nineteen was seeing my dad die of heart disease at forty-seven. This may be anecdotal evidence, but I believed that his meat-centric diet shortened his life. Many people told me at the time I became a vegetarian that I didn't need to worry about heart disease because I was a woman. It's been interesting over the four decades since my dad's death to see how many solid scientific studies have associated meat consumption with statistically greater risks of cancer and heart disease, particularly in women. For example, a ten-year-long National Cancer Institute study of more than five hundred thousand Americans published in *The Archives of Internal Medicine*, indicated that women who ate larger amounts of red meat had a 20 percent greater risk of dying of cancer and a 50 percent greater risk of dying of heart disease than women who ate little red meat.[7]

---

5   Although most of the products are fairly high in sodium, please keep in mind that many of the meat analogue sausage products, for example, are actually lower in sodium than their meat-based counterparts.

6   An Pan, "Red Meat Consumption and Mortality," *Archives of Internal Medicine,* published online March 12, 2012, accessed March 24, 2012. http://archinte.ama-assn.org/cgi/content/full/archinternmed.2011.2287

7   Tiffany Sharples, "The Growing Case Against Red Meat," Time, March 23, 2009, accessed March 24, 2012, http://www.time.com/time/health/article/0,8599,1887266,00.html

I'll get off my soapbox. If you've gotten this far in my book, you're hopefully receptive to the idea of cutting back your meat consumption. The purpose of this section is to provide you with information about the ten sources of meat analogues used in this book. I've developed all of the recipes in this book myself over the past seven years based on the products that I was able to find in my local grocery stores and health food stores. I deliberately avoided going on the websites of any of the companies that produce meat analogues until I finished my recipes and began writing this section of the book because I didn't want to be influenced by the recipes they might have published. The information I've included comes from the labels of each product and from the companies' websites. I have presumed that the information contained on each company's website is accurate and has been verified by that company.[8] I'm providing it in my book because I think it's important to know the ingredients used, so that if you are allergic to soy, for example, you know what product lines to stay away from and what you can safely eat. Since I am not affiliated with any of these companies, I am simply recommending the products that my family likes and that work well with my recipes. There are many other products made by each of these companies, and I'd invite you to explore their other offerings if you are so inclined.

Here are the companies that make the meat analogues used in this book in alphabetical order:

Boca (http://www.bocaburger.com)

Boca produces soy-based meat analogues that also contain wheat gluten. The two products I use in my recipes (**Ground Crumbles** and **Original Chik'n Nuggets**) are both vegan. Boca products can be found in the freezer section of most grocery stores. Boca is endorsed by Weight Watchers and its product labels show the number of PointsPlus value per serving, in case that's important to you.

Based on information on Boca's website:

- Each 87-gram serving of **Boca Original Chik'n Nuggets** contains 180 calories, 14 grams protein, 3 grams dietary fiber, 500 milligrams sodium, 0 milligrams cholesterol, 7 grams total fat, 0.5 grams saturated fat, and 0 grams trans fat.

- Each 57-gram serving of **Boca Ground Crumbles** contains 60 calories, 13 grams protein, 3 grams dietary fiber, 270 milligrams sodium, 0 milligrams cholesterol, 0.5 grams total fat, 0 grams saturated fat, and 0 grams trans fat.

Delight Foods (http://www.delightsoy.com)

After a bit of sleuthing, I discovered that the wonderful vegan soy chicken nuggets we buy from Earth Fare, our local natural foods store, are actually made by a company called Delight Foods Inc. I had

---

8   One thing I observed in preparing this section is that manufacturers are constantly tinkering with their products. Calories, protein, fat, fiber, and sodium levels on many products changed on both the product packages and on the manufacturer's websites several times since I first drafted this section. In fact, there were many times where the product package I was holding in my hands differed from the information on the company's website. Perhaps this is a good thing, because it means that the manufacturers are trying to continue to improve the taste, texture, and quality of their products. So here comes my legal disclaimer. I've updated information again in late June 2012 from each company's website, but I am not responsible for any updates made on their websites or product labels after that date.

initially thought about removing the recipes that use these Nuggets because I was afraid they would be hard for people to find outside of the nine states served by Earth Fare.[9] However, the Delight Foods website indicates that its products are also available at Whole Foods. Since Whole Foods has many more stores than Earth Fare, I thought it was worthwhile to keep the recipes using Delight Soy Nuggets in my book. The Nuggets are a vegan product, with a good taste and chewy texture that is very meat-like when properly prepared. Please note that in addition to the soy in the product's name, the Nuggets also contains wheat, so they are not gluten-free. Also, despite their name, the Nuggets are actually flat, rather irregularly shaped pieces—almost like small pieces of chicken breast that have been pounded flat with a mallet.

According to the Delight Foods website:

- Each 55-gram serving (three pieces) of **Delight Soy Nuggets** contains 130 calories, 9 grams protein, 2 grams dietary fiber, 284 milligrams sodium, 0 milligrams cholesterol, 7 grams total fat, 1 gram saturated fat, and 0 grams trans fat.

Delight Foods is a North Carolina-based company. Check out its website for a list of the stores that carry its products and the restaurants that serve its products. You might also ask your local store or co-op to carry this brand so you can try it.

Field Roast Grain Meat Company (http://www.fieldroast.com)

Field Roast is a Seattle, Washington-based company that was established in 1997. The company makes a line of retail products, as well as a line of products aimed at the food service industry.

The three products from Field Roast that I use in my recipes are the company's three vegetarian grain meat sausage products: **Italian Sausage**, **Mexican Chipotle Sausage**, and **Smoked Apple Sage Sausage**. All its sausage products are vegan and contain wheat gluten, but none contain soy. I like the fact that I can recognize all of the ingredients on the product labels, and don't see any listed chemicals or preservatives. I also think that the combination of seitan (wheat gluten) with vegetables, spices, and herbs is intriguing from the standpoint of both taste and texture.

Based on information on the Field Roast website:

- Each 92-gram serving (one sausage) of **Field Roast Italian Sausage** contains 240 calories, 25 grams protein, 4 grams dietary fiber, 570 milligrams sodium, 0 milligrams cholesterol, 10 grams total fat, 1 gram saturated fat, and 0 grams trans fat.

- Each 92-gram serving (one sausage) of **Field Roast Mexican Chipotle Sausage** contains 250 calories, 23 grams protein, 4 grams dietary fiber, 520 milligrams sodium, 0 milligrams cholesterol, 12 grams total fat, 1 gram saturated fat, and 0 grams trans fat.

---

9   Earth Fare is a natural foods store based in Asheville, North Carolina. It has stores in Alabama, Florida, Georgia, Indiana, Kentucky, Ohio, North Carolina, South Carolina, and Tennessee. A few months before this book went to press, Oak Hill Capital Partners acquired an 80% stake in Earth Fare, which may signal a new phase of expansion into other states. "Earth Fare Buyer Eyes Growth," Super Market News, April 16, 2012, accessed July 22, 2012, http://supermarketnews.com/retail-amp-financial/earth-fare-buyer-eyes-growth

- Each 92-gram serving (one sausage) of **Field Roast Smoked Apple Sage Sausage** contains 240 calories, 26 grams protein, 3 grams dietary fiber, 600 milligrams sodium, 0 milligrams cholesterol, 10 grams total fat, 1 gram saturated fat, and 0 grams trans fat.

You may find it challenging to find Field Roast products, but please ask for them in your local health food store. Some stores put them in the refrigerated section of the produce department, while others carry them in the freezer section. In one store, I found them in the "prepared foods" section along with salsa and hummus, which really surprised me. Field Roast makes excellent, good tasting sausages, which to my palette have the same texture and mouth feel as real meat. I look forward to the greater availability of Field Roast products as the company continues to widen its distribution channels.

Gardein (http://www.gardein.com)

Gardein products are manufactured by Garden Protein International, Inc. and are made in Canada. The company's meat analogues use soy, wheat, and pea proteins, along with vegetables and a combination of ancient grains (kamut, amaranth, millet, and quinoa). The company's website indicates that the ingredients are mostly non-genetically modified organisms (GMOs) and that it uses some organic ingredients in its products. Some of its products are frozen and others are found in the refrigerated produce section. I've been very pleased with the texture of Gardein products and am hoping that my local grocery will start carrying more of its product line. So far, I have only cooked with the **Lightly Seasoned Chick'n Scallopini**, the **Home Style Beefless Tips**, **Chick'n Fillets**, and the **Chick'n Strips**, but all of them have been very good.

Based on information from the Gardein website:

- Each 71-gram serving (one cutlet) of **Gardein Lightly Seasoned Chick'n Scallopini** contains 110 calories, 14 grams protein, 2 grams dietary fiber, 340 milligrams sodium, 0 milligrams cholesterol, 4.5 grams total fat, 0 grams saturated fat, and 0 grams trans fat.

- Each 100-gram serving of **Gardein Beefless Tips** contains 150 calories, 18 grams protein, 3 grams dietary fiber, 400 milligrams sodium, 0 milligrams cholesterol, 5 milligrams total fat, 0 milligrams saturated fat, and 0 grams trans fat.

- Each 100-gram serving of **Gardein Chick'n Filets** contains 160 calories, 19 grams protein, 2 grams dietary fiber, 370 milligrams sodium, 0 milligrams cholesterol, 7 grams total fat, 0 grams saturated fat, and 0 grams trans fat.

- Each 67-gram serving of **Gardein Chick'n Strips** contains 100 calories, 19 grams protein, 1 grams dietary fiber, 170 milligrams sodium, 0 milligrams cholesterol, 1.5 grams total fat, 0 grams saturated fat, and 0 grams trans fat.

Lightlife (http://www.lightlife.com)

Lightlife started in 1979 making a single product: tempeh. I remember seeing it in a Cleveland health food store and being excited about having a source for tempeh outside of Ann Arbor. In 1985, Lightlife began making Tofu Pups, a vegetarian hot dog which was one of my first experiences with meat analogues. Suddenly, I didn't feel like an outcast at cookouts with my husband's family, because I finally had something to eat that looked like their real meat on the grill. I use a lot of Lightlife products in my recipes because they are relatively easy to find in my local grocery and health food stores. Some of the products are vegan, but some contain egg white powder, so please check the labels carefully if this is important to you. All of the products contain soy and wheat gluten. The products I use in my recipes are **Gimme Lean Beef**, **Gimme Lean Sausage**, **Smart Ground Original**, **Smart Ground Mexican**, **Smart Cutlets Original**, **Smart Strips Chick'n**, **Smart Strips Steak**, **Smart Sausages Italian Style**, **Smart Sausages Chorizo Style**, and **Smart Bacon**.

Based on information from the Lightlife website:

- Each 57-gram serving of **Lightlife Gimme Lean Beef** contains 70 calories, 7 grams protein, 2 grams dietary fiber, 350 milligrams sodium, 0 milligrams cholesterol, 0 grams total fat, 0 grams saturated fat, and 0 grams trans fat.

- Each 57-gram serving of **Lightlife Gimme Lean Sausage** contains 60 calories, 7 grams protein, 3 grams dietary fiber, 310 milligrams sodium, 0 milligrams cholesterol, 0 grams total fat, 0 grams saturated fat, and 0 grams trans fat.

- Each 55-gram serving of **Lightlife Smart Ground Original** contains 70 calories, 12 grams protein, 3 grams dietary fiber, 310 milligrams sodium, 0 milligrams cholesterol, 0 grams total fat, 0 grams saturated fat, and 0 grams trans fat.

- Each 55-gram serving of **Lightlife Smart Ground Mexican** contains 70 calories, 9 grams protein, 3 grams dietary fiber, 310 milligrams sodium, 0 milligrams cholesterol, 0 grams total fat, 0 grams saturated fat, and 0 grams trans fat.

- Each 85-gram serving (one cutlet) of **Lightlife Smart Cutlets Original** contains 110 calories, 17 grams protein, 3 grams dietary fiber, 360 milligrams sodium, 0 milligrams cholesterol, 0.5 grams total fat, 0 grams saturated fat, and 0 grams trans fat.

- Each 85-gram serving of **Lightlife Smart Strips Chick'n** contains 80 calories, 14 grams protein, 4 grams dietary fiber, 520 milligrams sodium, 0 milligrams cholesterol, 0 grams total fat, 0 grams saturated fat, and 0 grams trans fat.

- Each 85-gram serving of **Lightlife Smart Strips Steak** contains 80 calories, 14 grams protein, 5 grams dietary fiber, 560 milligrams sodium, 0 milligrams cholesterol, 0 grams total fat, 0 grams saturated fat, and 0 grams trans fat.

- Each 85-gram serving (one sausage) of **Lightlife Smart Sausages Italian Style** contains 140 calories, 13 grams protein, 1 gram dietary fiber, 500 milligrams sodium, 0 milligrams cholesterol, 7 grams total fat, 1 gram saturated fat, and 0 grams trans fat.

- Each 85-gram serving (one sausage) of **Lightlife Smart Sausages Chorizo Style** contains 140 calories, 12 grams protein, less than 1 gram dietary fiber, 590 milligrams sodium, 0 milligrams cholesterol, 8 grams total fat, 1 gram saturated fat, and 0 grams trans fat.

- Each 10-gram serving (one strip) of **Lightlife Smart Bacon** contains 20 calories, 2 grams protein, 0 grams dietary fiber, 140 milligrams sodium, 0 milligrams cholesterol, 1 gram total fat, 0 grams saturated fat, and 0 grams trans fat.

MorningStar Farms (http://www.morningstarfarms.com)

MorningStar Farms products are probably the easiest to find in most areas of the United States. The company is now owned by Kellogg Company, which explains its wide distribution network. MorningStar Farms evolved from Worthington and Loma Linda, which were the only companies I know of that made vegetarian meat analogues prior to the 1970s. I have a few vegetarian friends who swear by Worthington products like FriPats and who still buy them in bulk. However, because I don't have a ready source for those products, I haven't cooked with them. My exposure to MorningStar Farms products began in the mid-1980s, when the MorningStar Farms brand began to be marketed more heavily. Initially, quite a few of my early recipes for this book used MorningStar Farms products. However, as different types of meat analogues became available, I experimented with them and in many cases, found that my family preferred the newer products. My sense, from reading their labels, is that MorningStar Farms products seem to contain a lot more ingredients that I don't immediately identify as "food." In contrast, the products I began using by companies such as Field Roast, Lightlife, Quorn, Tofurky, and Gardein contain fewer ingredients and seem less processed to me. I still think that MorningStar Farms makes some very good products, so this observation is not meant as a criticism of the company or its products. If MorningStar Farms is the only brand you can easily find in your grocery store, you will probably still get decent results using its products in many of my recipes. The two MorningStar Farms products which are featured in this book are **MorningStar Farms Veggie Bacon Strips** and **MorningStar Farms Meal Starters Grillers Recipe Crumbles**. Neither of these products is vegan and both contain soy and wheat. However, MorningStar Farms makes a number of vegan products, so if you are a vegan, some of its product offerings may work well for you.

Based on information from the MorningStar Farms website:

- Each 16-gram serving of **MorningStar Farms Veggie Bacon Strips** (2 strips) contains 60 calories, 2 grams protein, 1 gram dietary fiber, 230 milligrams sodium, 0 milligrams cholesterol, 4.5 grams total fat, 0.5 grams saturated fat, and 0 grams trans fat.

- Each 55-gram serving of **MorningStar Farms Meal Starters Grillers Recipe Crumbles** contains 80 calories, 10 grams protein, 3 grams dietary fiber, 230 milligrams sodium, 0 milligrams cholesterol, 2.5 milligrams total fat, 0 grams saturated fat, and 0 grams trans fat.

Quorn (http://www.quorn.us)

Quorn is made by a United Kingdom company that launched the brand in 1985. Its website claims that Quorn is the number one retail brand of meat-free foods in the world. The Quorn brand was introduced in the United States in 2002, and quickly became one of our family's favorite meat analogues. Unlike most other brands of meat analogues, Quorn products are not made with soy, so they are suitable for people who are allergic to soy. Two of their products (**Quorn Chik'n Tenders** and **Quorn Grounds**) are gluten-free, but the company's website indicates that they are made in a facility that processes gluten products. Moreover, since Quorn products contain a small amount of egg white, they are not suitable for someone who is a strict vegan.

The unique ingredient in Quorn products is mycoprotein, a type of edible fungi, similar to mushrooms, truffles, and morels. Mycoprotein is high in protein and contains all nine essential amino acids. Quorn products are found in the freezer section.

The Quorn products I use in my recipes are **Quorn Naked Chik'n Cutlets**, **Quorn Chik'n Nuggets**, **Quorn Chik'n Tenders**, **Quorn Grounds**, and **Quorn Turk'y Roast**.

Based on information from the Quorn website:

- Each 69-gram serving (one cutlet) of **Quorn Naked Chik'n Cutlets** contains 80 calories, 11 grams protein, 2 grams dietary fiber, 420 milligrams sodium, 0 milligrams cholesterol, 2.5 grams total fat, 0.5 grams saturated fat, and 0 grams trans fat.

- Each 85-gram serving of **Quorn Chik'n Nuggets** (about three or four nuggets) contains 180 calories, 10 grams protein, 2 grams dietary fiber, 460 milligrams sodium, 0 milligrams cholesterol, 8 grams total fat, 1 gram saturated fat, and 0 grams trans fat.

- Each 85-gram serving (about one cup) of **Quorn Chik'n Tenders** contains 80 calories, 10 grams protein, 4 grams dietary fiber, 390 milligrams sodium, 0 milligrams cholesterol, 2 grams total fat, 0.5 grams saturated fat, and 0 grams trans fat.

- Each 85-gram serving (about two-thirds cup) of **Quorn Grounds** contains 90 calories, 13 grams protein, 5 grams dietary fiber, 170 milligrams sodium, 0 milligrams cholesterol, 2 grams total fat, 0.5 grams saturated fat, and 0 grams trans fat.

- Each 90-gram serving of **Quorn Turk'y Roast** contains 90 calories, 14 grams protein, 5 grams dietary fiber, 470 milligrams sodium, 0 milligrams cholesterol, 1.5 grams total fat, and 0 grams trans fat.

Tofurky (http://www.tofurky.com)

Tofurky products are made by a company called Turtle Island Foods, based in Hood River, Oregon that started in 1980. Although the company makes a lot of different products, the three I use in my recipes are **Tofurky Beer Brats**, **Tofurky Sweet Italian Sausage with Tomato and Basil**, and **Tofurky Kielbasa**. I like its sausage products because they are vegan, made with organic soybeans and/or organic tofu, and contain no preservatives. The three products I use in my recipes contain both wheat and soy. I used to have to hunt for Tofurky products in the Carolinas, but now I am able to easily find them in many grocery stores. I hope the company continues to expand its distribution channels and broaden its product base.

Based on information from the Tofurky website:

- Each 100-gram serving (one sausage) of **Tofurky Beer Brats** contains 260 calories, 27 grams protein, 5 grams dietary fiber, 620 milligrams sodium, 0 milligrams cholesterol, 13 grams total fat, 1 gram saturated fat, and 0 grams trans fat.

- Each 100-gram serving (one sausage) of **Tofurky Italian Sausage** contains 270 calories, 29 grams protein, 8 grams dietary fiber, 620 milligrams sodium, 0 milligrams cholesterol, 13 grams total fat, 1.5 grams saturated fat, and 0 grams trans fat.

- Each 100-gram serving (one sausage) of **Tofurky Kielbasa** contains 240 calories, 26 grams protein, 8 grams dietary fiber, 660 milligrams sodium, 0 milligrams cholesterol, 12 grams total fat, 1 gram saturated fat, and 0 grams trans fat.

Trader Joe's (http://www.traderjoes.com)

According to its website, Trader Joe's is a specialty retail grocery store that began in Pasadena, California as Pronto Market in 1958 and became Trader Joe's in 1967.

The only meat analogue I'm currently using from Trader Joe's is **Trader Joe's Soy Chorizo**. I was surprised that I couldn't find nutritional information on Trader Joe's website, so I had to obtain this information from http://www.caloriecount.com.

- Each 70-gram serving of **Trader Joe's Soy Chorizo** contains 140 calories, 9 grams protein, 4 grams dietary fiber, 700 milligrams sodium, 0 milligrams cholesterol, 10 grams total fat, 1.5 grams saturated fat, and 0 grams trans fat.

WestSoy (http://www.westsoytofu.com)

WestSoy is part of the Hain Celestial Group, Inc., a large holding company that owns a ton of brands you would probably recognize: Celestial Seasonings Tea, Arrowhead Mills, Greek Gods Yogurt, Earth's Best Baby Food, Hain Pure Foods, Health Valley, Imagine Foods, and many, many others. WestSoy makes seitan products that are relatively easy to find in many stores. Seitan is made with wheat gluten, which puts it on the must avoid list for folks who are gluten intolerant, but it has no soy, which is great for people who are allergic to soy. The two products I use in my recipes are **WestSoy Cubed Seitan** and **WestSoy Seitan Strips**.

According to the WestSoy website:

- Each 85-gram serving of **WestSoy Cubed Seitan** contains 120 calories, 21 grams protein, 1 gram dietary fiber, 320 milligrams sodium, 0 milligrams cholesterol, 2 grams total fat, 0 grams saturated fat, and 0 grams trans fat.

- Each 85-gram serving of **WestSoy Seitan Strips** contains 120 calories, 21 grams protein, 1 gram dietary fiber, 320 milligrams sodium, 0 milligrams cholesterol, 2 grams total fat, 0 grams saturated fat, and 0 grams trans fat.

There is a lot more information on the website of each company about its corporate practices, the nutritional content of its products, and the way its products are made. If you decide to try additional products or need specific information, I'd suggest checking out the websites for more details.

Here is a convenient chart that shows the products I use in this book, so that you can determine at a glance what you can use if you have dietary restrictions.

Product	Soy	Wheat Gluten	Mycoprotein	Vegan
Boca Chik'n Nuggets	✔	✔	✘	✔
Boca Ground Crumbles	✔	✔	✘	✔
Delight Soy Nuggets	✔	✘	✘	✔
Field Roast Italian Sausage	✘	✔	✘	✔
Field Roast Mexican Chipotle Sausage	✘	✔	✘	✔
Field Roast Smoked Apple Sage Sausage	✘	✔	✘	✔
Gardein Lightly Seasoned Chick'n Scallopini	✔	✔	✘	✔
Gardein Beefless Tips	✔	✔	✘	✔
Gardein Chick'n Filets	✔	✔	✘	✔
Gardein Chick'n Strips	✔	✔	✘	✔
Lightlife Gimme Lean Beef	✔	✔	✘	✔
Lightlife Gimme Lean Sausage	✔	✔	✘	✔
Lightlife Smart Ground Original	✔	✔	✘	✔
Lightlife Smart Ground Mexican	✔	✔	✘	✔
Lightlife Smart Cutlets	✔	✔	✘	✘
Lightlife Smart Strips Chick'n	✔	✔	✘	✘
Lightlife Smart Strips Steak Style	✔	✔	✘	✘
Lightlife Smart Sausages Chorizo Style	✔	✔	✘	✘
Lightlife Smart Sausages Italian Style	✔	✔	✘	✘
Lightlife Smart Bacon	✔	✔	✘	✔
MorningStar Farms Veggie Bacon Strips	✔	✔	✘	✘
MorningStar Farms Meal Starters Grillers Recipe Crumbles	✔	✔	✘	✘
Quorn Naked Chik'n Cutlets	✘	✔	✔	✘
Quorn Chik'n Nuggets	✘	✔	✔	✘
Quorn Chik'n Tenders	✘	✘	✔	✘
Quorn Grounds	✘	✘	✔	✘
Quorn Turk'y Roast	✘	✘	✔	✘
Tofurky Beer Brats	✔	✔	✘	✔
Tofurky Italian Sausage	✔	✔	✘	✔
Tofurky Kielbasa	✔	✔	✘	✔
Trader Joe's Soy Chorizo	✔	✘	✘	✔
WestSoy Cubed Seitan	✘	✔	✘	✔
WestSoy Seitan Strips	✘	✔	✘	✔

Please check out my website, http://www.foolacarnivore.com, for my own color photos of many of the dishes in this book, along with my blog and new featured recipes. The website also includes nutritional information, links to helpful websites, and other features that were hard to include in a book.

Vegan Recipes – We have flagged recipes in the Index that are vegan, and there are many others which can be made into vegan dishes with minor modifications (like substituting soy margarine for butter, eliminating cheese, or substituting soy cheese). Although I sometimes cook vegan meals, I love dairy products (especially cheese and yogurt) too much to completely eliminate them from my diet. Jenny

Ford, the helpful young woman who prepared my index, tells me that Daiya makes a surprisingly good shredded soy cheese mozzarella, as well as a palatable shredded cheddar. She tells me that the Daiya products are vegan, gluten free, melt well and don't have an unpleasant aftertaste. While soy cheese will never replace dairy cheese in my home, Daiya products may be an alternative worth exploring for vegans who want to try some of my recipes that contain cheese.

Trademark Symbols – The tension between Nancy, the fledgling author, and Nancy, the attorney, was never more evident than in my stubborn retention of registered and unregistered trademark symbols for all the companies and products mentioned in this book up until the last version of my manuscript. I had a number of friends who read early versions of my manuscript tell me that my exacting use of the ™ and ® symbols was over-the-top and distracting. Finally, Ann, my editor at CreateSpace cited Rule 8.152 from *Chicago Manual of Style,* 16th Edition, to persuade me that there was no legal requirement to use the symbols and that they should be eliminated whenever possible. Since lawyers love rules, I was relieved that Ann finally gave me a solid reason to remove them from a recognized source.

OTHER INGREDIENTS

- **Onions** — In the Carolinas, it is very easy to find Vidalia onions, Peruvian sweet onions, Texas onions, or another variety of sweet onion on a year-round basis. I think they impart a lighter, sweeter flavor to my cooking. I particularly look forward to the arrival of the Baby Vidalia onions (which look like scallions on steroids) in early February at my local farmers' market. However, I recognize that sweet onions may not be readily available in many regions of the country. So, if sweet onions are hard to find in your locale, please substitute white or yellow storage onions, and you will still get excellent results.

- **Tomatoes** — When I use canned tomatoes, I normally reach for Muir Glen Organic Tomatoes. According to information on the package labels and the Muir Glen website (http://www.muirglen.com), the tomatoes are field grown and ripen on the vine using certified organic practices. I frequently use Muir Glen Organic Fire Roasted Tomatoes because they give a deeper, richer, smokier flavor to my sauces. I think that they can make almost any dish taste meatier. The Muir Glen website indicates that the company is transitioning to cans with non-BPA liners for the 2012 harvest.[10] The other brand I like is Pomi, an Italian brand which has no citric acid, no salt, and no preservatives. I use Pomi for a lot of my Easy Weeknight Dinners; since they have no added water, they cook very quickly. I use Pomi Chopped Tomatoes and Pomi Strained Tomatoes. Both products come in a box, rather than a can, and the company's website (http://www.pomi.us.com) indicates that the aseptic packaging is recyclable and BPA free. Watch the use-by dates carefully. While the company claims that its products have a long shelf life, the dates by which you need to use the tomatoes seem much shorter to me than the canned varieties.

- **Pasta** — There are several brands of pasta that we enjoy: De Cecco, Barilla and Colavita. We particularly like the Barilla Plus Multigrain pasta, which is similar in taste to white flour pasta, but is a bit firmer and heartier. It is made with a grain and legume flour blend (with lentils, chick peas, spelt, barley, flax-seed, and oats). According to the package, each serving delivers four grams of fiber and ten grams of protein. Although it does not contain whole wheat flour, we prefer it to Barilla Whole Grain pasta. We also like the lovely small pasta shapes that Barilla makes under its new brand, Piccolini. Although Piccolini looks like white pasta, it has some added whole wheat flour, which Barilla claims provides three times more fiber than regular white pasta. Piccolini currently comes in three shapes: mini penne, mini rotini, and mini conchiglie (shells). When I have specified small pasta shapes in a recipe, I've generally used the Barilla Piccolini pasta. If you are gluten intolerant, there are a number of good gluten-free pastas on the market—most of which I have not tested because no one in my family has that dietary restriction.[11]

- **Cheese** — I know that cheese has a lot of fat, but I simply adore cheese. I tried macrobiotics for a couple of years in the late 1970s and kept craving cheese. I finally decided that my Sicilian heritage could not be denied, and went back to eating dairy products. Cheese is a key ingredient in many of my recipes, and it's important that you use good quality cheeses.

---

10   http://www.muirglen.com/news/n-10.aspx

11   *Cook's Illustrated* published the results of an interesting taste test of various gluten-free pastas in the March, 2005 issue. http://www.cooksillustrated.com/tastetests/results.asp?docid=10033. However, many new brands have entered the market since the article was published, so I think an updated evaluation by this magazine is long overdue.

- **Parmigiano-Reggiano** — A lot of what passes for "cheese" in our country is horrible. I'm referring to the ubiquitous green cans of nasty white flakes that many people use for "Parmesan cheese." When I specify Parmesan, I almost always use Parmigiano-Reggiano. I buy a large chunk when it's on sale for $9.99 per pound and then feel thrifty when I see the price skyrocket back up to $20.00 or more per pound. It will last a long time if you only grate the amount needed for a recipe. There are only a few regions in Italy (mostly in Emilia-Romagna) where the cheese can be legitimately labeled as "Parmigiano-Reggiano" and you need to check the rind of the cheese to make sure that it carries that stamp. If you can get it freshly cut off the huge wheel, it will smell heavenly and taste even better. Once you've experienced the sharp, complex, nutty flavor of Parmigiano-Reggiano, you'll wonder why you ever used anything else in Italian cooking.

- **Other Grana Cheeses** — The term Grana refers to a type of hard, mature cheese which has kind of a granular texture and is good for grating. In some preparations, I like the sharp saltiness of Pecorino Romano instead of the more subtle, nutty flavor of Parmigiano-Reggiano. Pecorino is made with sheep's milk, and it is often a bit less expensive than Parmigiano-Reggiano. I definitely prefer it to domestic Romano cheese. The other two Grana cheeses I occasionally use are Asiago and Grana Padano. Asiago is made with cow's milk and is a bit sweeter and milder. Make sure you buy imported Asiago, because many of the versions made in the United States that I've sampled are rather bland. Grana Padano is a wonderful, complex cheese, but because of its cost, I would reserve it for a special cheese plate instead of grating it over pasta.

- **Mozzarella** — I became a fresh mozzarella snob during the five years we lived in Baltimore in the mid-1990s. I was spoiled by the fresh mozzarella we bought every Saturday from Mastellone Deli and Wine Shop. Sweet Mr. Mastellone would get up every morning at five o'clock to make the most impeccably fresh mozzarella I've ever tasted. If you have a source for fresh mozzarella, such as a local grocer in an Italian-American neighborhood, don't even think about buying the pre-packaged version sold in your supermarket. Fresh mozzarella is made with cow's milk and is called *fior di latte*. Don't confuse it with the expensive imported mozzarella packed in water or brine and made from the milk of water buffalo, which is what most people living in Italy would use. If you don't have a reliable local source for fresh mozzarella, I've had decent results with Sorrento mozzarella. Don't waste your money on pre-grated mozzarella.

- **Goat Cheese** — I buy Bosky Acres goat cheese at our farmers' market from a local goat creamery in Waxhaw, North Carolina.[12] They make a lemon-pepper variety and a garlic-chive variety that are my family's favorites. However, there are probably great local goat cheeses available in your area. Most goat cheeses are fresh[13] and fairly perishable, so fresh, local goat cheese is always better than an aging piece of imported chèvre languishing in the back of the dairy case.

- **Ricotta** — Like goat cheese and mozzarella, a locally made fresh creamy ricotta is always better than a mass-produced ricotta. It should be smooth, sweet, and creamy. It is highly perishable, so don't let it languish in your fridge.

---

12   Read about them at http://www.boskyacres.com.

13   There are also aged goat cheeses, but they are very expensive, and are more for after dinner cheese plates than for cooking. The goat cheese that I specify in my recipes is always a soft, unripened, white, spreadable fresh cheese.

- ○ **Cheddar** — I like Cabot Cheeses a lot, particularly Cabot Seriously Sharp White Cheddar. Cabot Creamery is a 1,200 farm family dairy cooperative with members in New England and upstate New York.[14]

- **Olive Oil** — When I specify olive oil in a recipe, I always mean a good quality extra virgin olive oil. Olive oil comes in many different grades. Extra virgin olive oil is from the first pressing of the olives, and has a free oleic acid count of less than one percent.[15] I look for cold-pressed olive oil, and prefer olive oils from Italy or Spain. Make sure you check the label for the date it was pressed, rather than just the "sell by" date. Often, when a good quality extra virgin olive oil is marked down, it may be because it is a bit past its prime, although still within its "sell by" date. You can spend a lot of money on a great olive oil, just as you can with a bottle of great wine. However, I don't think that is necessary for everyday use. I use Colavita or Filippo Berio as my extra virgin olive oil for most daily cooking purposes, and save the expensive, single-source, handpicked extra virgin olive oils for salads or for very special dishes. If you are interested in learning more about olive oil, I can't think of a better place to start than Ari Weinzweig's wonderful book, *Zingerman's Guide to Good Eating*.

- **Wine** — Never cook with a wine that you wouldn't drink with your dinner. I am always amazed by the people in my local grocery store who stop me and ask where they can find "cooking wine." I explain to them that the wines labeled as "cooking wine" contain salt and are absolutely foul. Most recipes only require one-quarter to one-half cup of wine, so that's not too much from your bottle, is it? The other benefit is that the food you're eating will contain the subtle flavor and aroma from the wine you used to make the dish. Then, when you're sitting at the table, enjoying the meal and the wine, your taste buds will recognize the connection between the food and what you're drinking. I personally consider wine to be more of a food than a beverage. My husband and I drink wine almost every night with our dinner. I know that many people don't imbibe and that this practice may make us decadent in the eyes of many people. However, when I've spent the time and effort to make a delicious home-cooked meal, we want to relax and enjoy our time together, particularly now that our son is in college. If you don't drink wine and just need some wine for cooking, I suggest buying a decent bottle of dry vermouth to use when recipes call for a small amount of dry white wine. Risotto, for example, will taste very different if it is made without wine or vermouth, because it will lack the proper balance of acidity. If you object to using wine even in cooking, you can always add stock or a mixture of stock and white grape juice. However, I haven't personally tested any of my recipes with that modification — so you're on your own.

- **Salt** — Most of my recipes specify sea salt. Since sea salt is made from evaporated seawater, it is less processed than regular table salt. Sea salt also contains minerals from the evaporated water that change its taste, and sea salt will taste different depending on its source. The flavor profile of a sea salt from Italy, for example, is quite distinctive when compared to the French *fleur de sel*. Since the nutritional differences are slight and sea salt is definitely more expensive, you may prefer to use iodized table salt or kosher salt. (Never use expensive sea salt to salt your pasta water. I usually add two tablespoons of kosher salt when the water is at a rolling boil, but regular table salt will work fine, too.) You'll notice that most of my recipes do not specify the amount of salt to use. I do this for three reasons. First, all the meat analogues contain a lot of sodium. I've found that I can add just a

---

14   http://www.cabotcheese.coop/pages/about_us/index.php
15   Ari Weinzweig, *Zingerman's Guide to Good Eating* (Boston: Houghton Mifflin Company, 2003), 2–29.

tiny bit of salt or none at all, and the finished dish is well seasoned. Second, I cook for my mother who is on a low sodium diet, so I have become very sensitive to the unnecessary addition of salt in many recipes. In fact, I particularly taste it when I eat out at restaurants, and often find the excess salt to be strong and unpalatable. Third, I rarely add salt during the actual cooking process, although I know that most cooks do because it is supposed to add layers of flavor. I simply taste my dish when it's done cooking, and add a very small amount of sea salt only if I think it is needed to enhance the overall flavor of the dish. I see salt as a highly personal preference, so please add or decrease salt to suit your taste and the health needs of your family.

- **Stock or Broth** — I use either stock or broth in my recipes, but both are always vegetable-based. Since there are no bones to simmer to make a vegetable stock, I guess I'm usually making a broth. I simply think of stock as having a more concentrated and complex flavor than broth. Frankly, I think that the difference between vegetable stock and broth is probably a matter of semantics. Here's my best tip if you want to avoid the expensive, high sodium versions of vegetable stock and broth that are sold in the stores. I have been making a mean Potato Peel Broth from *The Vegetarian Epicure*[16] for over thirty-five years. Please check out Anna Thomas' simple recipe for an easy way to turn potato peels and a few assorted vegetables into an inexpensive broth that will serve as a flavorful basis for the sauces in this book. While Wolfgang Puck's versions of vegetable stock and broth are both very good, they cost at least $3.00 per quart and are much higher in sodium than my Potato Peel Broth. Why not economize by making your own Potato Peel Broth from stuff that you would normally throw away? I usually buy vegetable stock or broth from Wolfgang Puck, Earth Fare, or Imagine only if I don't have my own Potato Peel Broth handy. However, when I'm super-efficient, I can make a big pot of Potato Peel Broth while I'm doing laundry or working in my office at home, and then freeze the broth in quart size containers so that I have a ready supply whenever I need it in a recipe.

- **Herbs** — I grew up gardening every summer at Miles School Gardens in the Cleveland Public Schools Garden Program. Later on in high school, I worked as a student assistant and always tried to pull "herb duty" at the school's herb garden with my best friend, Patty Frost, during long summer afternoons. From that experience, I learned that growing herbs is easier and more rewarding than most people imagine. Many herbs will grow well even in poor soil and will come back year after year. I feel particularly blessed living in the southeastern United States. In Fort Mill, South Carolina, most of my herbs (except for basil, dill, and fennel) re-seed and return every spring, and a few of them (like bay, mint, rosemary, and thyme) enliven my cooking all year long. We've created six small raised beds in our back yard that are filled with herbs. When we lived in Baltimore, we grew herbs in big whiskey barrels and other containers that we could effectively shelter from the cold. With a small investment of time and energy, you can be blessed with healthy organic herbs in your cooking for a fraction of the cost of buying fresh herbs at the market or grocery store. Please see the Bibliography for several good books about herbs.

Here are the herbs I grow and use in my recipes:

- ○ **Italian Parsley** (also known as flat-leaf parsley) — I adore Italian parsley and use it almost every day. Since I make so many Italian dishes, it is the most popular herb in my kitchen (with basil

---

16   Anna Thomas, *The Vegetarian Epicure* (New York, Vintage Books, 1972), 50.

running a close second). Once you start cooking with fresh parsley, you'll notice a fresher, more delicate taste in your cooking. I almost never use dried parsley. In my geographic region, both Italian parsley and curly parsley are biennial, which means that they will grow for two years in a normal life cycle. I let the plants flower in the second year and allow the seeds to fall to the ground. The following year, I always have new parsley plants (but often not in the bed in which the mother plant lived). I watch for the volunteers, dig them up, and move them back where they belong.

- **Curly Parsley** — Although I use curly parsley less than I do Italian parsley, it is still a staple in my herb garden. Because I like the stronger flavor of Italian parsley, I tend to use the curly leaf parsley more as a garnish, or add it after I'm done cooking to dress the dish, which intensifies its flavor.

- **Basil** — I grow a lot of basil because I make a ton of pesto. However, an average family needs only three or four plants to enjoy basil all summer long. Be sure to wait until all chance of frost is over before you plant your basil outside. I sometimes get impatient and plant it too early and then lose my precious basil plants to a late frost. There are an increasing number of basil varieties, and I've tried many of them. However, I still prefer the common sweet basil or Genovese basil which grows well in most climates and produces lots of glossy green leaves. Pinch back your basil frequently to encourage growth, never pinching mid-stem, but always right above the next set of leaves. As I mention in my pesto recipe, don't use the flowering tops of your basil plants or your pesto will taste nasty. I also like to tear my basil, rather than cutting it with a knife, because the knife makes it brown quickly.

- **Mint** — I love mint, but it takes over a garden. Grow it in its own separate bed or container, and be vigilant about weeding out any volunteers that wander outside of those confines. There are many different varieties of mint, but they will cross- pollinate, so it's hard to keep their distinctive fragrance and taste pure unless you have plenty of room to plant them far apart. My suggestion is to just plant peppermint or spearmint in its own separate bed or container, and let it go wild. Cut it back to the ground when the stems get woody, and it will just sprout up again. It is almost impossible to kill mint!

- **Oregano** — Oregano, like mint, is a perennial and very hard to kill. I grow it year-round. Since it goes well with tomatoes, it appears in a lot of my recipes.

- **Rosemary** — Rosemary is one of my favorite herbs. I have two large rosemary bushes and use rosemary in a lot of my chicken analogue recipes and some of my dishes that use Italian sausage analogues.

- **Bay** – The sweet bay I planted fourteen years ago soon became a shrub and now is actually a seven-foot tree. I use bay leaves in a lot of my recipes, and especially like to use them fresh, rather than dried. Since my sweet bay tree is so large, it's never a problem for me to prune a few branches to keep in water in my kitchen in case I'm too lazy to go out to the herb garden while I'm cooking.

- ○ **Thyme** — Thyme is another perennial that I use almost daily. I grow several different varieties, and have not had a problem with cross-pollination. I especially like lemon thyme, English thyme, and a new variety that has a larger leaf and tastes like a mixture of thyme and marjoram. Thyme will spread quickly, so you only need a couple of plants.

- ○ **Dill** — Dill can be tough to grow because it goes to seed so quickly. Whatever you do, don't plant it close to fennel or it will cross-pollinate. Some years I find it easier to just buy a bunch of fresh dill at the market every other week. I put it in a large glass of water and cover it with a plastic bag secured with a rubber band. It will keep in your refrigerator for a week or two, provided you change the water every couple of days.

- ○ **Fennel** — Please don't confuse the herb fennel with the vegetable fennel (finocchio) that is an ingredient in many of my dishes. When you are growing fennel as an herb, you're using the leaves or fronds. If you're growing it as vegetable, you're probably growing a variety known as Florence fennel, and you'll be using the bulb. Fennel has a smell a little like licorice and I think it's a delightful plant to have in your garden. Again, please don't plant it near dill or it will cross-pollinate.

- ○ **Chives** — Chives are an easy plant to grow almost all year long. In the late spring and early summer, chives produce a beautiful pale purple flower that grows in clusters and looks a little like a pin cushion. I think that these chive blossoms make a lovely garnish.

- ○ **Sage** — I enjoy fresh sage, but I have been less successful growing it than my other herbs. Our Carolina summers are so hot that sage doesn't do well. I plant it in late summer or early fall. This strategy helps the plant avoid our withering summer heat and gives us fresh sage for all our hearty fall and winter dishes.

COOKING TOOLS

Since I've been cooking for many years, I have a very well-equipped kitchen. However, if you are just starting out as a cook, there are a few essential tools that you should consider. They don't have to cost you a fortune, and sometimes you can pick up an older model for a song at a yard sale.

Here are the tools I suggest you consider acquiring to make cooking easier and more pleasurable:

- **<u>Food Processor</u>** — I still have the Cuisinart food processor I received from my mom as a wedding present. It was a fairly expensive piece of equipment back then, but it's still in good working condition after almost thirty years. My advice is to buy a good quality food processor[17] with a bowl capacity of no less than seven or eight cups and a motor that can stand up to tough jobs and a lot of use. It continues to vie with my slow cooker as my most used piece of kitchen equipment.

- **<u>Slow Cooker</u>** — I honestly didn't think I would like using a slow cooker, until I received a free one for being a loyal shopper at my local grocery store. It was a fairly inexpensive model with just high and low settings. After using it for a few weeks, I wondered how I'd ever gotten along without one. A couple of years ago, I replaced it with a programmable model by Cuisinart, which gives me the ability to time recipes more exactly, along with simmer and warm settings. Like my first model, it has a removable ceramic insert, which is an indispensible feature for easy clean up. In all of my slow cooker recipes I suggest using liners for easy clean up. The only brand I'm aware of is Reynolds Slow Cooker Liners. While I try to minimize the use of anything disposable in my kitchen, I know that I also wasted a lot of soap and water cleaning baked-on food from my slow cooker. The liners may look like plastic, but they are made of a food-safe nylon resin. They fit three to six-and-a-half quart round and oval slow cookers and have been a huge timesaver for me. I just wish that I'd been smart enough to invent them!

- **<u>Stand Mixer</u>** — I used a small hand mixer for many years, and finally became frustrated with its limitations. My Kitchenaid stand mixer was a birthday gift from my sweet husband back in the early 1990s. It is still working like a champ over 20 years later. Kitchenaid is constantly updating its mixers with new colors and features, but I am content with my old four-and-a-half quart tilt-head "classic series model which still sells for under $200. I don't think you need a lot of fancy attachments or the high-end model that lifts up the bowl. You really only need three attachments, all of which come with the standard model: the paddle that you will use 80 percent of the time, the whisk, and the dough hook. Once you use a stand mixer for my meatball recipe, you'll never want to mix by hand again.

- **<u>Scale</u>** — I have a small electronic scale by Salter that allows me to accurately measure foods, either in ounces or grams. Many times, I just "eye ball" measurements. If the package of cheese is eight ounces, and I need three ounces, I just cut off what looks to be the right amount. However, in trying to be more precise about measurements for this book, I found myself frequently using the scale. If you are watching your weight or consider yourself a novice cook, a scale can really help you judge the amount of ingredients you need with more precision.

---

17   Kitchenaid also makes a good food processor.

- **Measuring Cups and Spoons** — Just as with the scale, a good set of measuring cups and spoons will help you improve your ability to measure ingredients until you get comfortable with measuring things by eye. You also need to be aware that there is a difference between measuring liquid and dry ingredients. I recommend getting a set of metal measuring cups for dry ingredients and one-cup and four-cup glass or heavy plastic measures for liquid ingredients. My old Pyrex four-cup measure finally gave up the ghost, because the lip was cracked and the markings were almost completely erased from years of use. My husband replaced it one Christmas with a plastic OXO four-cup measure that has two sets of markings, so I can accurately assess how much is in the cup when I look at it from either the top or the side.

- **Cast Iron Heat Diffuser** — I grew up cooking on a gas stove, and I still enjoy cooking on a gas cook top. This simple cast-iron circle diffuses heat and eliminates hot spots. When I say in a recipe to cook something over low heat, I'm almost always using my heat diffuser. Mine is a very old seven-inch model made by Ilsa, an Italian company, and I probably bought it for just a few bucks. Amazon sells a similar Ilsa model with a stainless steel handle for about $16. This is one of my most frequently used pieces of kitchen equipment, and is well worth the modest investment.

- **Garlic Press** — For many years, I stubbornly minced garlic and refused to use a press. About a year ago, I finally bought a garlic press, and was pleasantly surprised at the difference between pressed and minced garlic and how easy the press was to clean. Most garlic presses can handle unpeeled garlic cloves, which saves time. I've found that since I stopped mincing and started pressing that the garlic breaks down more completely and its flavor permeates the entire dish. There are a lot of great garlic presses on the market and *Cook's Illustrated* did an excellent evaluation of two dozen models in its July, 2007 issue.[18] If you're used to mincing, you might be surprised at how much more convenient it is to use a garlic press.

- **Microplane** — For many years I used a Zyliss rotary cheese grater until I discovered the joys of grating hard grana-type cheeses on a Microplane grater. I bought the zester/grater model, which is extremely versatile, and use it almost every day. Make sure to store it in the plastic sleeve that serves as a protective cover because the tiny blades are extremely sharp.

---

18   http://www.cooksillustrated.com/equipment/overview.asp?docid=10670

FOOL A CARNIVORE

...WHO LOVES GROUND MEAT!

THE LASAGNA THAT STARTED IT ALL

This is the lasagna recipe that is the star of my introduction—the one that gave me the confidence that I really could fool carnivores. When I was putting the finishing touches on this book, I realized that I had never written it down. I have made many versions of lasagna, and can almost make it in my sleep. The two keys are (a) using the Barilla Lasagna sheets (rolled flat like homemade) that don't required pre-boiling (or another brand of no-boil lasagna noodle), and (b) making plenty of sauce, because the lasagna sheets need to soak up the hot sauce in order to cook properly. This lasagna is wonderful re-heated. In fact, it even gets better after a day or two. I usually end up with leftover ricotta mixture, which I bake to accompany another meal. Put the leftover ricotta mixture in lightly greased individual ramekins, sprinkle it with parmesan and panko[19] (or bread crumbs), and pop it in the oven after the lasagna has been cooking for about thirty minutes. It makes a wonderful breakfast or light lunch.

Please note that I've created a more healthy option in this recipe, using reduced fat ricotta and mozzarella. If you don't care about fat or calories, consider using full fat ricotta and mozzarella. The creamy texture is worth the difference in taste. Please don't ever use pre-grated mozzarella. You actually pay more and get a poorer quality cheese that is coated with chemicals to keep it from sticking.

1–2 tablespoons extra virgin olive oil
1 large onion, chopped
4 garlic cloves, pressed
28-ounce can crushed tomatoes
28-ounce can organic diced tomatoes with basil
2 bay leaves
¼ cup fresh basil
¼ cup chopped fresh parsley
¼ cup dry white wine, optional
Freshly ground black pepper
¼ teaspoon sea salt
1 tablespoon extra virgin olive oil
12-ounce package Lightlife Smart Ground Original
1 package Field Roast Italian Sausage, quartered lengthwise and chopped into small pieces
4 ounces fresh spinach
3 eggs

---

19   Panko is Japanese-style bread crumbs. The crumbs are more coarsely textured and crispier than traditional bread crumbs. My preferred brand is Ian's. I like them because the crumbs are made with unbleached whole wheat flour and do not contain sugar, which is an unnecessary ingredient that a lot of brands contain.

20-ounce container of ricotta cheese (reduced fat)
1 cup parmesan cheese, grated
2 cups reduced fat mozzarella, grated
Freshly grated nutmeg
Freshly ground black pepper
12–15 sheets of no-boil lasagna (depending on whether you end up doing 3 or 4 layers)
2–3 cups reduced fat mozzarella, grated

1. Heat the olive oil and sauté the chopped onion over moderately low heat until softened and translucent, about 6–7 minutes. Add the garlic and sauté for a minute, then add the tomatoes and herbs. Simmer for about 30 minutes, adding a little white wine or tomato juice if it looks too thick.

2. While the sauce is cooking, make the meat layer. Heat the tablespoon of olive oil in a separate skillet and sauté the Smart Ground for 3 minutes. Add the Italian sausage pieces, and sauté for another 2 minutes.

3. While the sauce is cooking, steam the spinach for 3–4 minutes. Squeeze out all the green juice (saving it, of course, for stock), chop it, and set aside on a triple layer of paper towels to cool.

4. Get a large mixing bowl, break in the eggs and beat them with a whisk. Add the ricotta, parmesan, mozzarella, chopped spinach, nutmeg, salt and pepper, and mix well.

5. Preheat the oven to 375°F. Now, you get to be an architect! Lightly coat a large, deep 11 x 13-inch baking dish with olive oil or non-stick cooking spray. Ladle in about a cup of the hot sauce.

6. Add a layer of lasagna noodles. Cover with about ⅓ of the ricotta mixture (or ½ of it if you are only making three layers instead of four), and then sprinkle with either ⅓ or ½ of the Smart Ground and Italian sausage. Sprinkle some of the mozzarella over the Smart Ground and Italian sausage, and then ladle sauce over the top.

7. Repeat step 6 at least once more (or twice if you have enough sauce remaining).

8. For your last layer, end with the lasagna noodles and cover with all the remaining sauce. Cover tightly with foil and bake for 45 minutes.

9. When the timer goes off, remove the foil, add the remaining mozzarella, and put the dish back in the oven for another 15–20 minutes.

10. Take the lasagna out of the oven and let it rest for at least ten to fifteen minutes before you try to cut it into portions. Make a salad and have a lovely glass of Cabernet or Chianti Classico while you smell the aroma and anticipate how delightful it will taste.

Serves 10–12

PASTA WITH BOLOGNESE SAUCE

Every Italian family makes its own version of "Sunday gravy." This recipe could have just as easily gone in my sausage chapter, but the consistency of the ground meat in the sauce stands out more than the sausage does. A couple of ingredients may give you pause, but please use them. The bread and milk mixture is the key to the sauce's consistency and the finely minced mushrooms provide a depth of flavor that I wasn't able to achieve using the just the Smart Ground and Tofurky sausages alone. I use brown crimini mushrooms or baby portobello mushrooms, but even if you can only find white button mushrooms, the sauce will still be tasty. We enjoy this dish with a hearty Sangiovese or Zinfandel.

28-ounce can crushed tomatoes
28-ounce can diced tomatoes
1 onion, diced
3 tablespoons extra virgin olive oil (divided use)
6–8 mushrooms
3–4 cloves garlic, minced or pressed
1 slice Italian or French bread
2 tablespoons milk
12-ounce package of Lightlife Smart Ground Original
Sea salt and freshly ground black pepper
2 Tofurky Italian sausages
2–3 bay leaves
Several sprigs of fresh basil
Several sprigs of fresh oregano
1-pound box spaghetti, linguine, or penne
Freshly grated Parmigiano-Reggiano cheese

1. Put a liner into the slow cooker. Add the crushed tomatoes and diced tomatoes, and begin cooking on high.

2. Dice onion in the food processor. Wipe out the bowl. Heat a large skillet, add 2 tablespoons olive oil, and begin sautéing the onion over moderate heat until translucent, about 6 minutes.

3. Wipe any dirt off the mushrooms with a paper towel. Never wash mushrooms with water, because it makes them mushy. Cut each cleaned mushroom in half and put them in the food processor. Pulse in short bursts—1 to 2 seconds—until the mushrooms are finely minced. Add the minced mushrooms to the onions and continue sautéing for another 5–6 minutes. Add the garlic to the sauté, and cook for another minute or two.

4. Add the onion and mushroom mixture to the tomatoes in the slow cooker, and season with a little sea salt and freshly ground black pepper. Wipe the skillet clean.

5. Wipe out the food processor bowl and add the bread, torn in quarters. Pulse in a few short bursts until you have coarse crumbs. Add the milk, a little more sea salt and freshly ground black pepper. Pulse again, then add Smart Ground, broken up into small chunks, and pulse until mixed. Heat your cleaned skillet again, add 1 tablespoon of olive oil, and sauté the Smart Ground mixture for 4–5 minutes until lightly browned before adding it to the pasta sauce in the slow cooker.

6. Slice the Tofurky Italian sausages in half lengthwise and then thinly slice them. Either sauté the sausage pieces in a little olive oil or add them directly to the simmering pasta sauce in your slow cooker–your choice, because both ways work well.

7. Add the bay leaves, basil, and oregano to the sauce, along with more salt and pepper as needed. (I save time by putting in the whole sprigs of herbs and then take them out later when I'm ready to serve.)

8. Cook for 5–6 hours on high or about 8 hours on simmer. Taste carefully and adjust seasoning. Remove the bay leaves and the other fresh herb sprigs, and serve over spaghetti, linguine, or penne with plenty of freshly grated Parmigiano-Reggianno.

Serves 6–8

Mexican Black Bean Chili

This is a super easy recipe that produces a great chili. This is a relatively new version which uses Lightlife Smart Ground Mexican Style. You can also use Smart Ground Original, if your family likes milder food. Please use any type of salsa that your family enjoys. Also, we use V8 in this recipe instead of tomato juice. When I want to spice things up, I use the V8 Spicy Hot, but sometimes use the low-sodium V8 if I want to cut back on salt for my mom.

I love the simplicity of making chili in the slow cooker, and the men in my family love its hearty, meaty texture. I also appreciate that chili cooking times in the slow cooker can be flexible. If you're short on time, you can cook it on high for three to four hours. Or, if you're making this before you leave for work, cook it on low for eight hours. I like to add the Smart Ground in the last hour of cooking, but if you know you are going to need to eat the minute you walk in the door from work, you can sauté it after the onions and peppers and add it before you leave for work. It will still be good, but the texture will be a little less "meaty." I've filmed a video of how to make this dish, so please watch it at http://www.ehow.com/ehow-food.

2 tablespoons extra virgin olive oil
1 large onion, coarsely chopped
1 medium red or yellow bell pepper, chopped into small ½-inch squares (1 cup of chopped peppers)
2 cloves garlic, minced or pressed (optional)
3 cups of cooked black beans or 2 16-ounce cans[20] black beans (drained and rinsed)
16-ounce jar salsa, mild or medium
12-ounce package Lightlife Smart Ground Mexican Style or Smart Ground Original
1 cup V8 or tomato juice (divided use)
Monterrey Jack or pepper Jack, grated

1. Heat a large skillet and add olive oil. Sauté onion for 5–6 minutes over medium heat. Add the bell pepper pieces and sauté for another 3–4 minutes. If you're using garlic, add it in the last minute, and turn the heat down a bit so that it doesn't burn.

2. While your onions and pepper are cooking, lightly oil your slow cooker or line it with a liner. Put in the rinsed black beans, the jar of salsa, and ½ cup of the V8 or tomato juice. Then add the sautéed onion, bell pepper and garlic. Cook on high for 3–4 hours or on low for up to 8 hours.

---

20 Cans of beans vary in size, depending on the brand. In my pantry, I have 15-ounce cans, 15.5-ounce cans, 16-ounce cans, and 19-ounce cans of black beans. The difference is relatively small, so it won't really matter which size you use in this recipe.

3. Sauté the Smart Ground in the same pan that you used for the onion and bell pepper. Sauté over low heat until lightly browned, about 4–5 minutes. Add to the slow cooker, along with the remaining ½ cup of the V8 or tomato juice and cook for another 30–60 minutes (depending on how much time you have). I sometimes add up to another half cup of V8 or tomato juice because we like a juicy chili. Please use less if you like a denser, meatier chili. Serve with grated Monterey Jack or pepper Jack cheese, accompanied by some crisp tortilla chips, salsa, and guacamole.

Serves 4–6

MEATY CORN BREAD SKILLET

Leftover corn bread is usually not a problem in my household. However, we occasionally make an enormous batch and have some left over. Normally, I transfer casseroles into proper baking dishes. However, watching my concoction simmering away on the stove, I decided to throw caution to the wind. I left everything in the skillet and put my corn bread topping right on top before popping it in the oven. Who doesn't like to save some precious clean up time? I've classified this as an Easy Weeknight Meal even though it takes thirty minutes to bake, because the prep time is less than fifteen minutes. While it's baking in the oven, you can make a large green salad and some guacamole, and relax a bit before dinner.

1–2 tablespoons extra virgin olive oil
1 medium onion, chopped
1 green bell pepper, chopped
3–4 garlic cloves, minced or pressed
16-ounce can kidney beans, drained and rinsed
12-ounce package MorningStar Farms Meal Starters Grillers Recipe Crumbles or 12-ounce package Quorn Grounds
3–4 fresh tomatoes, chopped
1 cup mild salsa
6 egg whites
1 whole egg
½ cup milk
4 cups crumbled leftover corn bread (check out my Southern Corn Bread recipe following Hoppin' John for a Crowd)
1½– 2 cups grated white cheddar cheese or pepper Jack cheese

1. Preheat oven to 350°F.

2. Heat a large skillet, add the olive oil, and sauté the onion for 5–6 minutes over medium heat. Add the bell pepper pieces and sauté for another 3–4 minutes, and then the garlic in the last minute of cooking so that it doesn't burn.

3. Add the kidney beans and sauté for a minute. Add the frozen meat analogue product you're using and sauté for 5–6 minutes until thawed.

4. Add the tomatoes and sauté for a few minutes. Then add the salsa.

5. Meanwhile, whisk together the egg whites, whole egg, and milk. Crumble the corn bread into the mixture. Add the grated cheese and mix until incorporated.

6. Cover the top of the simmering skillet with the corn bread mixture. Bake in the oven for 30 minutes.

Serves 6

Mexican Pizza

On a busy weekday evening, this is a fun alternative to ordering out for pizza, and almost as quick. I was out of mozzarella and didn't have time to make a fresh tomato sauce for pizza, because we were all ravenous. Instead of running out to the grocery store (or picking up the phone and ordering pizza), this recipe came together in a flash and was tasty and filling. Feel free to mix up the peppers and use different colors, depending on what you have on hand. I also don't specify a type of salsa, because you know what your family likes best. If you're using a pizza stone, make sure that it is on the lowest level of your oven.

1 can Pillsbury Pizza Dough (thick crust variety) or a ball of frozen pizza dough, thawed
7-ounces Lightlife Gimme Lean Beef or Sausage (½ the package)
1–2 tablespoons extra virgin olive oil
16-ounce jar salsa, mild or medium
½ cup diced green bell pepper
½ cup diced red bell pepper
½ cup diced yellow or orange bell pepper
¼–½ cup diced jalapeño peppers, optional
3–4 ounces pepper Jack cheese, grated
3–4 ounces white cheddar, grated

1. Preheat oven to 425°F. Roll out the pizza dough. Spray baking sheet lightly with non-stick cooking spray and put the pizza dough on the baking sheet.

2. Heat a skillet, and add the olive oil. Pinch small pieces of Gimme Lean Beef or Sausage and fry in hot olive oil. When browned, drain on several thicknesses of paper towels.

3. Meanwhile, spread salsa on the pizza dough. Top with diced peppers and sausage. Sprinkle cheeses on top.

4. Bake for 18–20 minutes. Let rest about 4–5 minutes before cutting into squares.

Serves 4–6

EASY TACO BAKE

Sometimes when I get home from work (and haven't been smart enough to set up the slow cooker before I left), I'm scrambling to feed a hungry husband and son in a very brief time. Fortunately, both my guys love Mexican food and this recipe can be ready in just 20 minutes. My husband Bill is a huge jalapeño fan, and Nick's taste runs to the mild side. This is a flexible recipe, because each of the ingredients comes in varying degrees of heat—so you can adjust as needed to suit your family's taste. You can use any kind of diced tomatoes, but we like the RO*TEL Original Diced Tomatoes and Green Chilies that come in 10-ounce cans. Check the label on the refried beans to make sure that they do not contain lard. I've made this with both refried pinto beans and refried black beans, and it is tasty with either type. A healthy side salad will round out the meal.

16-ounce can vegetarian refried beans
10-ounce can diced tomatoes (or 1¼ cups fresh diced tomatoes)
12-ounce package Lightlife Smart Ground or Smart Ground Mexican
1 tablespoon extra virgin olive oil
½ cup salsa (mild, medium or hot—your choice)
½ cup roasted red peppers, chopped (optional)
8 taco shells
8-ounces white cheddar cheese or pepper Jack, shredded
2 avocados, chopped
1 lime, juiced
Sea salt and freshly ground black pepper
Reduced-fat or non-fat sour cream
Additional salsa
Your favorite brand of white or yellow tortilla chips

1. Preheat oven to 350°F. Combine refried beans and tomatoes and spread in 11 x 13-inch baking dish that has been lightly oiled or coated with cooking spray.

2. Sauté the Smart Ground in a little olive oil until browned and add salsa and optional roasted red peppers.

3. Stuff the taco shells with the Smart Ground mixture and place the taco shells in mixture of refried beans and tomatoes. Stand the shells upright in the thick base formed by the refried beans and tomato mixture. Sprinkle the shells with cheese. Bake for 10 minutes.

4. While the tacos are baking, peel the avocados and chop into ½-inch pieces, adding lime juice, sea salt, and pepper to taste. Spoon chopped avocados over the hot tacos and serve with plenty of refried beans, sour cream, additional salsa, and tortilla chips.

Serves 4

Greek Stuffed Eggplant

I realize that many carnivores do not like eggplant, so if that describes the carnivores in your family, you may want to skip this recipe. On the other hand, those of you who appreciate Mediterranean food will probably love this recipe. A lot of recipes call for salting the eggplant, but if you use small, very fresh, just-picked eggplants, you can safely eliminate that step. I like to make this in individual baking dishes, but you can also use a large rectangular baking dish that fits your six eggplant halves. Serve it with pesto pasta. (Please see my Pesto Chicken for my favorite pesto recipe.) We really enjoy the pesto with orzo, the tiny pasta that looks like grains of rice, and shredded zucchini, sautéed with garlic, lemon, and mint. I'm not a big fan of Greek wines, so I served this meal with a delightful Spanish Rioja.

3 small eggplants
2 tablespoons extra virgin olive oil
Sea salt and freshly ground black pepper
2 cloves garlic, pressed or minced
7 ounces Lightlife Gimme Lean Beef (½ of the package), broken into pea-sized pieces
1 tomato, diced
10 mint leaves, minced
4 basil leaves, minced
8–10 oregano leaves, minced
¼ teaspoon fennel seeds
Sea salt and freshly ground black pepper
1 lemon, juiced
Feta cheese, crumbled
Pecorino Romano cheese, grated

1. Preheat oven to 375°F. Cut each eggplant in half, and using a melon ball scoop, scoop out the flesh. Leave about a ½-inch shell. Reserve the shells of eggplant. Dice or mince the eggplant flesh by hand or use a food processor.

2. Heat a large skillet and add the olive oil. When the oil is hot, sauté the eggplant flesh, adding a little more olive oil if needed. Cook until the eggplant is just starting to turn a golden brown color, add salt and pepper and set aside.

3. In a clean pan, heat the olive oil and sauté the garlic for a minute or so. Add the Gimme Lean pieces, and continue sautéing until they just start to brown, and then add the diced tomato. After 4–5 minutes, add the herbs, fennel seeds, sea salt, and pepper. Add the cooked eggplant to the skillet.

4. Lightly oil a casserole dish that is large enough to hold your eggplant shells or use individual oven-proof baking dishes. Stuff the eggplant shells with the eggplant/meat mixture and then squeeze a little lemon juice over them.

5. Cover tightly with aluminum foil and bake for 45 minutes.

6. Remove the aluminum foil, lower heat to 350°F, top with feta and Romano cheese and bake uncovered for an additional 15–20 minutes until bubbly and lightly browned.

Serves 6

COTTAGE PIE

I originally wanted to create a shepherd's pie that would give due credit to its British origins, but still have a fresh flavor—in other words, meaty enough to "pass," without being too meaty. The problem is that I'm not aware of a meat analogue that tastes like lamb, and as a friend's husband at a recent Oberlin College reunion reminded me, a true shepherd's pie needs to be made with lamb. I decided to re-invent this dish as more of a cottage pie, and think that either Boca Ground Crumbles or Quorn Crumbles work well. We made this post-Thanksgiving, so we had extra mashed potatoes for the topping, and served it with lovely collard greens, flavored with lots of garlic. Please make my Garlic Mashed Potatoes recipe if you don't have any mashed potatoes on hand. If collards don't appeal to you, please feel free to accompany this dish with green beans, broccoli, peas, or any other green vegetable that was left over from your holiday feast. I often make my own pie crust, but when I'm pressed for time, I find that the refrigerated Pillsbury pie crust is a good substitute. We enjoyed this dish with a hearty Cabernet Sauvignon, but I think a fine Malbec would work well, too.

1 unbaked pie crust, at room temperature
1–2 tablespoons extra virgin olive oil
1 onion, diced
2 stalks celery, sliced lengthwise into thin strips and diced
1 cup diced carrots
1 red bell pepper, diced
1 package Boca Ground Crumbles or Quorn Grounds
1 teaspoon Worcestershire sauce, optional[21]
1 teaspoon reduced-sodium soy sauce
¼–⅓ cup vegetable broth or stock
4–6 ounces cheddar cheese, grated
2 cups leftover mashed potatoes, warmed slightly, and thinned with a bit of milk or cream if they seem too thick to spread

1. Unroll and place the pie crust in a 10-inch pie pan. Prick the bottom in several places with a fork. Bake the pie crust at 425°F for 8–10 minutes until just starting to color.

---

21   Most commercially prepared Worcestershire sauce contains anchovies. If that bothers you, either omit the Worcestershire sauce, or use a vegan version. We've tried several and think that Annie's Natural Organic Worcestershire Sauce tastes closest to the real thing.

2. While the pie crust is baking, heat a large skillet and add the olive oil. Sauté the onion over moderate heat until translucent, followed by the celery, carrot, and red bell pepper. This should take about 8–10 minutes.

3. Add the frozen meat analogue, soy sauce, Worcestershire sauce, broth or stock, and sauté for 4–5 minutes more.

4. Remove the pie crust from the oven and cool on a wire baking rack. Lower the oven temperature to 400°F.

5. Layer half of the meat and veggie mixture over the cooled crust and sprinkle with half the cheese.

6. Add the remaining meat and veggie mixture, followed by the remaining cheese.

7. Top with the leftover mashed potatoes. Bake for 30 minutes.

Serves 4–6

MINI MEAT LOAVES

I know you're wondering how you can possibly create a passable meat loaf with meatless products. My suggestion is to make individual mini meat loaves. Preparation time is minimal if you use a food processor or a stand mixer. I like using individual oval baking dishes, with two mini meat loaves per dish. If you don't have individual baking dishes, you can also use a rectangular baking dish that will hold all of your mini meat loaves. Because the Gimme Lean products don't need to cook as long as real meat, your dinner will be ready in short order. An added bonus is that the individual mini meat loaves can be served right out of the oven, so you don't have to waste time waiting for a large meat loaf to cool slightly before slicing it. I usually serve this with my Garlic Mashed Potatoes recipe which can be easily made while the mini meat loaves are baking. Add a steamed green vegetable and a hearty Malbec or Shiraz. Your carnivores will love this recipe!

⅔ cup fresh bread crumbs (or crumbs made from16 saltines or another mild cracker)
¼ cup milk
1 egg
¼ cup finely chopped fresh parsley
½ teaspoon sea salt
Freshly ground black pepper
2 cloves garlic, pressed
2 tablespoons Worcestershire sauce[22]
2 teaspoons Dijon mustard
14 ounces Lightlife Gimme Lean Beef
14 ounces Lightlife Gimme Lean Sausage
1 cup canola oil
1½ cups ketchup
5 tablespoons apple cider vinegar
½ cup brown sugar
1–2 tablespoons Worcestershire sauce

1. Preheat oven to 400°F.

2. Pulverize the saltines (or slightly stale bread) in your food processer to make fine crumbs.

---

22   Most commercially prepared Worcestershire sauce contains anchovies. If that bothers you, either omit the Worcestershire sauce, or use a vegan version. We've tried several and think that Annie's Natural Organic Worcestershire Sauce tastes closest to the real thing.

3. Put the crumbs in a large bowl (or stand mixer) and add milk and egg. Mix well. Season with fresh parsley, sea salt, freshly ground black pepper, garlic, Worcestershire Sauce, and Dijon mustard and mix again. Add Gimme Lean Beef and Gimme Lean Sausage, and mix thoroughly.

4. Shape into small oblongs, 1½ x 3-inches. The mixture should make about 8 to 10 mini meat loaves.

5. Fry each mini meat loaf in canola oil, turning carefully to brown each side. Drain on a triple thickness of paper towels after each side is nicely browned.

6. While the mini meat loaves are cooking, make your sauce by stirring together the ketchup, apple cider vinegar, brown sugar, and Worcestershire sauce in a small bowl. Divide the sauce, reserving half for your table.

7. Lightly oil the individual baking dishes or rectangular baking dish with oil or cooking spray, and put in your mini meat loaves. Spoon half of the sauce over the mini meat loaves. Bake for 30 minutes at 400°F. Serve with the reserved sauce and Garlic Mashed Potatoes.

Serves 4–5

GARLIC MASHED POTATOES

Here is my never fail, greatly loved recipe for garlic mashed potatoes. This side dish is simple, yet so addictive! I generally use russet potatoes, because they have a lot of starch and are low in moisture. Russets cook fairly quickly, and mash well. I've also had good results with Yukon Gold potatoes, which have a bit less starch than the russets. If you are using Yukon Gold potatoes, please cook the potatoes about five to eight minutes longer than I've suggested for the russets, so that they will mash easily. Some garlic mashed potato recipes will tell you to toast (or roast) the garlic and then add it to the potatoes once they are cooked. I've tried this technique, but I think that boiling the garlic with the potatoes adds a subtler flavor. I've also found it to be faster and easier, so please, give it a try.

The order in which the butter and dairy are added really does matter. According to an article in the September-October, 2000 issue of *Cook's Illustrated*[23], when the butter is added before the dairy, the fat coats the starch molecules, and gives you silkier, creamier mashed potatoes. When I've experimented and tried adding the dairy first, the potatoes were heavier and tasted pasty instead of creamy. As with a lot of things in life, this is meant to be a flexible recipe, so you may need to adjust the unsalted butter and dairy a bit, depending on the size of your potatoes. By the way, although I have a ricer and five different types of potato mashers, my favorite potato masher is actually a pastry cutter. It fits in my hand well, and although unconventional, it works like a charm for me.

6–8 russet potatoes, about 2 pounds
6–10 garlic cloves (papery covering removed, but cloves left whole)
½ teaspoon sea salt
2–3 bay leaves
Freshly ground black pepper
½ cup (1 stick) unsalted butter, melted
1 cup milk or half-and-half, heated

1. Peel the potatoes and put in cold water as you work. (Save the peelings for making vegetable broth or consider composting them.) Drain off the cold water, and quarter the potatoes. Put the potatoes, garlic cloves, salt and bay leaves in an appropriately sized pot and add just enough water to barely cover everything. Cover the pot and bring to a boil.

2. Boil about 15–20 minutes or so until the potato pieces are tender and easily pierced by a fork.

---

23   Dawn Yanagihara, "Garlic Mashed Potatoes," *Cook's Illustrated*, September–October 2000: 10–11.

3. Here's where some of the flexibility comes in. I sometimes only drain off a portion of my cooking water, because I think it imparts a wonderful flavor with almost no calories. This simple trick allows me to add a lot less butter and half-and-half. However, assuming you want to drain off all the cooking water (saving it for potato peel broth–of course), do so and begin adding the melted unsalted butter a few tablespoons at a time while you mash. Add small amounts of the heated milk or half-and-half until a smooth consistency is obtained, along with freshly ground black pepper and more sea salt if needed. (If I've used some of the potato cooking water, I may only add ½ cup of milk or half-and-half, eliminating a lot of fat and calories.)

Serves 4–6

SWEDISH MEATBALLS

We have a dear friend, Bjorn Vikard, who Bill and I met scuba diving in Australia in 1997. Bjorn has proven to be a life-long friend, and not just a "dive acquaintance," and through him we have learned a lot about Swedish food and culture. My husband enjoyed Bjorn's version of Swedish Meatballs (with real meat) and raved about them, so I decided to figure out how to make a meat analogue version. I first made this dish on a snowy Saturday in January, 2010 when the Carolinas were blasted by a freak winter storm. Bill and Nick were speechless at how good it was—in fact, Nick called it "grand slam." This is a delicious, hearty dish that deserves a really fine Pinot Noir. Recently, we enjoyed it again with a 2008 Diamond Ridge Pinot Noir from Santa Barbara County. Serve with Garlic Mashed Potatoes (the recipe follows my Mini Meat Loaves), Swedish Cucumbers (which immediately follows this recipe), and blackberry preserves. Bjorn tells me that lingonberry preserves are traditional in Sweden, but IKEA stores are the only place I've found to buy lingonberry preserves in the United States. To our American palates, my homemade blackberry preserves were a fine accompaniment.

1 egg
1 slice bread, torn into very small pieces and buzzed in the food processor
7 ounces Lightlife Gimme Lean Sausage (½ of the package)
7 ounces Lightlife Gimme Lean Beef (½ of the package)
½ small onion, grated or finely minced
⅛ teaspoon allspice
⅛ teaspoon freshly grated nutmeg
1 teaspoon brown sugar
Freshly ground black pepper
½ teaspoon sea salt
1 teaspoon baking powder
Canola oil
2–3 tablespoons unsalted butter
2–3 tablespoons unbleached all-purpose white flour
1½ cups vegetable stock, warmed in a small sauce pan
1 tablespoon brown sugar
⅓–½ cup whole milk, half-and-half, or light cream
2 teaspoons fresh lemon juice
½ teaspoon sea salt
Freshly ground black pepper

1. Lightly beat the egg, and add the breadcrumbs. Add the meat analogues, onion, allspice, nutmeg, brown sugar, black pepper, sea salt, and baking powder. Either mix by hand with

a wooden spoon or in your stand mixer on low speed until thoroughly combined. After everything is thoroughly mixed, form into golf-ball-sized spheres and fry in about 1½ inches of hot canola oil until nicely browned on all sides. Drain on a triple thickness of paper towels.

2. Melt the butter in a sauce pan over low heat. Add flour to make a roux[24] to thicken the sauce. Cook the roux for a minute or two before adding the warmed stock. Cook your sauce until reduced by half to a third, and then add the brown sugar.

3. Add the milk, and cook the sauce for a few more minutes until it coats a spoon. Add the lemon juice, salt and pepper.

4. Cook the sauce for a few minutes. Add your meatballs and cook for at least 5–8 minutes until heated through.

Serves 4-6

---

24   A roux is the basis for many classic sauces. A roux thickens your sauce and is made by simply cooking equal amounts of flour and butter for a few minutes over low heat to eliminate any raw flour taste. The roux is now ready for you to add a warmed liquid to it–in this case, stock.

SWEDISH CUCUMBERS

4 Kirby cucumbers
½ cup white vinegar
½ cup sugar
⅛ teaspoon allspice
¾ teaspoon sea salt
Freshly ground black pepper

1. Peel and slice your cucumbers. Put them in a bowl.

2. Boil the vinegar and sugar over medium heat until the sugar is completely dissolved. Season the vinegar mixture with allspice, sea salt and pepper.

3. Pour the vinegar mixture over the cucumbers and cover them with plastic wrap. Let it sit for at least 30 minutes, while you're making the meatballs and sauce.

4. Serve the cucumber salad in small bowls to accompany the Swedish Meatballs.

Serves 4-6

MEATY MEATBALLS

I have tried a number of the pre-made meatballs, some of which are pretty darn good (the version made by Quorn comes to mind) and most of which are not to my family's liking. I decided to make my own meatballs, and wow, what a difference in flavor and texture! This recipe might seem daunting, but it only takes about forty minutes of prep time and can be on your table in about an hour. You may wonder why I don't mix the meatballs in my food processor since I had to use it to make the bread crumbs. The reason I don't just make the meatballs in the food processor is that mine isn't powerful enough to stand up to the denseness of this mixture. I seem to get better results mixing by hand or using the stand mixer. Serve with buttered orzo or another small pasta, and a green vegetable, like shredded zucchini with garlic, lemon, and mint.

1–2 tablespoons extra virgin olive oil
1 onion, finally chopped
1–2 cloves garlic, minced or pressed
28-ounce can fire roasted crushed tomatoes
28-ounce can ground peeled tomatoes or crushed tomatoes
1 bay leaf
3–4 tablespoons fresh basil leaves, minced
2–3 tablespoons fresh parsley, minced
Sea salt and freshly ground black pepper
1 cup fresh bread crumbs, made from French or Italian bread
14-ounce package Lightlife Gimme Lean Beef
14-ounce package Lightlife Gimme Lean Sausage
1 egg
1 clove garlic, minced or pressed
2 tablespoons grated Parmesan cheese
1 tablespoon minced fresh rosemary leaves
2 teaspoons minced fresh basil leaves
1 tablespoon minced fresh parsley
Sea salt and freshly ground black pepper
Canola oil
½ pound fresh mozzarella
½–¾ cup freshly grated Parmesan

1. Make your tomato sauce first, so that it is bubbling away while you form and cook your meatballs. Heat a large sauce pan, add the olive oil, and sauté the onion for 5–6 minutes, until soft and translucent. Add the garlic and sauté for a minute more. Add both cans of

tomatoes, bay leaf, and herbs. Simmer over moderately low heat for about 20 minutes. Taste and correct seasonings with salt and pepper.

2. Make the bread crumbs in the food processor. Put the bread crumbs and all the other meatball ingredients in the bowl of your stand mixer, or just mix by hand. Mix until all the ingredients are thoroughly incorporated.

3. Form your meatballs into golf ball-sized spheres and brown them on all sides in hot canola oil. Drain them on a triple thickness of paper towels.

4. Coat a large baking dish with olive oil or a non-stick cooking spray. Add half of the tomato sauce, then add the meatballs, and cover with the remaining tomato sauce. Top with the mozzarella and Parmesan. Bake at 400°F for 15–20 minutes.

Serves 6–8

CLASSIC SPAGHETTI AND MEATBALLS

Who in their right mind doesn't love this classic comfort dish that we all lovingly remember from childhood? The problem is that it is too often made with a bottled sauce that drenches every square inch of the pasta and contains meatballs that strike a single note—namely, ground beef. Good meatballs come from a variety of ingredients and should have a fresh taste. I've made these meatballs with my own homemade fresh bread crumbs and with panko—both are very good as a binder. If you decide to use panko, give them a quick buzz in the food processor first, so they will be a bit smoother in texture. I bake the meatballs in the oven, so there is no added fat. Consequently, this dish is much lower in fat and calories than a traditional recipe. Isn't it nice to be able to satisfy your craving for one of the simple pleasures from childhood without expanding your waistline? If you're serving wine, consider a Sangiovese or a Zinfandel. Serve with plenty of freshly grated Parmigiano-Reggiano, crusty Italian bread, and a green salad.

1 tablespoon extra virgin olive oil
½ onion, diced
2 garlic cloves, pressed
28-ounce can crushed tomatoes
16-ounce can diced fire roasted tomatoes
¼ cup dry white wine
2–3 tablespoons fresh Italian parsley, minced
2–3 tablespoons fresh basil, minced
2–3 tablespoons fresh oregano, minced
Sea salt and freshly ground black pepper to taste
¾ cup dried bread crumbs or panko (see note above)
⅓ cup buttermilk or plain low fat yogurt
1 egg
14-ounce package Lightlife Gimme Lean Beef
7 ounces Lightlife Gimme Lean Sausage (½ the package)
¼ cup Parmesan cheese, grated
1 garlic clove, minced or pressed
2 tablespoons fresh Italian parsley, minced
Sea salt and freshly ground black pepper
1-pound box spaghetti
Freshly grated Parmigiano-Reggiano

1. To make the sauce, heat a large sauce pan, add the olive oil, and sauté the diced onion for 5–6 minutes, until translucent. Add the garlic and sauté for another minute or two. Make sure not to let the garlic brown.

2. Add the tomatoes, wine, parsley, basil, oregano, sea salt, and pepper. Cover and let simmer for about 30–45 minutes while you make your meatballs.

3. Line a baking sheet with non-stick aluminum foil and preheat oven to 400°F.

4. Mix together the bread crumbs and buttermilk or yogurt and let sit for a few minutes.

5. In a large mixing bowl, beat the egg, then add the breadcrumb mixture, and all the remaining ingredients. You can either mix the meatballs by hand or use the stand mixer. Just make sure that all the ingredients are thoroughly incorporated.

6. Form the meatballs into golf ball-sized spheres or slightly smaller. You should have about 35–40 meatballs.

7. Bake the meatballs on the foil-lined baking sheet for 20 minutes. After 20 minutes, flip them and bake for another 5–10 minutes.

8. Let the tray of meatballs cool on a wire rack for about 10 minutes. Put the meatballs in the sauce for 8–10 minutes to warm them, while you make your spaghetti in a big pot of boiling salted water. Cook the spaghetti according to the package directions until al dente. Drain the spaghetti in a colander, and then put it in a large serving bowl. Pour several ladles of sauce over the top and toss to incorporate. Serve in pasta bowls with extra sauce and meat balls on top. Sprinkle with freshly grated Parmigiano-Reggiano.

Serves 6

Fool A Carnivore

...Who Loves Sausage!

BAKED ITALIAN SAUSAGE, FENNEL, AND PEPPERS OVER PEPPERY PARMESAN POLENTA

This is a very easy recipe with flexible proportions. I have classified it as a Weekend Dinner because it takes almost an hour to properly make the polenta. I start by making the polenta first, and while it is cooking, I assemble and begin sautéing the other ingredients. It really helps if you can enlist a family member to help you stir the polenta. My husband is a strong and patient polenta stirrer (remember, polenta is just another name for Southern grits), and even our son was willing to help when he was younger. I think kids love to get involved with cooking, but you need to put them in charge of something for which they are completely responsible. Just remind a younger child to keep a hand (protected by an oven mitt) on the sauce pan handle as he or she stirs. I don't recommend buying the rolls of pre-made polenta as a short cut. Not only is it very expensive, it just isn't as tasty as the polenta you can make yourself. I recently updated this recipe with Field Roast Italian Sausage because I love that product's taste and texture. Depending on my audience, I use different cheeses. If you're making this dish for kids, use mozzarella and plenty of it. On the other hand, use fresh goat cheese if you're serving this for an adult dinner party.

I've filmed a video of how to make this dish, so please watch it at <u>http://www.ehow.com/ehow-food</u>.

2 tablespoons extra virgin olive oil, plus a little more for coating the baking pan
1 medium onion, coarsely chopped
1 red bell pepper, sliced into 2-inch matchsticks
1 yellow bell pepper, sliced into 2-inch matchsticks
1 fennel bulb, tops and base removed, quartered lengthwise, cored and thinly sliced
1–2 cloves garlic, minced or pressed
½ cup dry white wine or vermouth
½ cup vegetable stock
28-ounce can diced tomatoes
½ cup chopped fresh tomatoes
1 teaspoon fennel seeds
1 bay leaf
2 large fresh rosemary sprigs
3–4 Field Roast Italian Sausages, casings removed
Sea salt and freshly ground black pepper
¾ pound mozzarella, grated or 6–8 ounces fresh goat cheese
1 recipe Peppery Parmesan Polenta, below

1. Preheat oven to 400°F. Lightly coat a large baking dish with a little olive oil or cooking spray.

2. If you have an extra hand to stir, prepare the polenta (recipe follows) while the fennel is cooking and put it in the prepared baking dish once it is fully cooked.

3. Heat a large skillet and add the olive oil. Sauté the onion over low heat 5–6 minutes. Add the peppers, fennel, and garlic and sauté 6–8 minutes more. Add the wine and stock and cook down until the liquid has reduced by half or about 10–12 minutes.

4. Add tomatoes, fennel seeds, bay leaf, rosemary sprigs, salt, and pepper. Cover and simmer for about 10 minutes. (Keep stirring that polenta!)

5. Slice all of the sausages into ½-inch slices and add to the simmering pan. Cook for about 5–8 minutes – make sure the liquid is mostly evaporated.

6. Pour the contents of the skillet over the polenta. Bake for 15 minutes.

7. If you're making this for kids, sprinkle with grated mozzarella and bake for 5 more minutes. If you're making this for adults, remove the baking dish from the oven and dot the top with small pieces of fresh goat cheese.

Peppery Parmesan Polenta

I've filmed a video of how to make this polenta, so please watch it at http://www.ehow.com/ehow-food.

3 cups boiling water (and up to an additional cup of boiling water as you stir)
1 teaspoon sea salt
1 cup corn grits
2 tablespoons unsalted butter
Freshly ground black pepper
½ cup grated Parmigiano-Reggiano cheese

1. Put the first 3 cups of water in a sauce pan and bring it to a boil. Add the salt, and then pour the corn grits into the boiling water in a steady stream.

2. Stir like your life depends on it. It's so easy for polenta to develop lumps. So even though some recipes say you can cover it and leave it alone for awhile, every time I've done so, I've had a lumpy mess. You will probably need to cook it for 45 minutes to an hour, depending on the coarseness of the grits. (I like to use stone ground grits which will take a much longer time to cook than a more refined variety.) I start adding additional water after about 10–12 minutes, adding about ¼ cup at a time. You want your polenta mixture to be thick, but not so thick that you can't continue to stir. When the texture seems smooth and creamy, add the unsalted butter, plenty of freshly ground black pepper, and parmesan. Stir well, and then pour in a thin layer into a well-greased baking pan. Quickly smooth out with a spatula so you have a thin, even layer of polenta and then let it set for about 10–15 minutes.

3. If you don't want to work so hard, you can double the recipe and make the polenta in the slow cooker. Cook it for an hour on high, and then 7–8 hours on low, stirring occasionally. I'd like to acknowledge Crescent Dragonwagon for her inspired idea about how to make polenta in the slow cooker without the elbow grease.[25]

Serves 6–8

---

25   Crescent Dragonwagon, *Passionate Vegetarian* (New York: Workman Publishing, 2002), 444.

ORECCHIETTE WITH SAUSAGE AND CAULIFLOWER

I've created two different versions of pasta with cauliflower and sausage, since we love the combination so much. It's amazing what varying the proportions of the vegetables, changing the pasta, and using a different type of sausage can mean to the taste of a well-loved dish. In this version, I use orecchiette, which means "little ears" in Italian. They are small, rounded, bowl-like shapes that are sturdier than most pastas and perfect for cradling the sauce. I cut the sausage on a mandoline in thin, even slices, and sauté them until they are lightly browned. The smaller amount of cauliflower in the sauce in this recipe puts more emphasis on the sausage.

½ head of cauliflower, separated into small florets
4 tablespoons extra virgin olive oil (divided use)
1 onion, chopped
2 cloves garlic, minced
28-ounce can diced tomatoes
½ cup dry white wine
1 large sprig of rosemary, finely minced
2 Tofurky Italian sausages, thinly sliced in ¼-inch rounds on a mandoline
2–4 tablespoon vegetable stock or broth (or more wine)
1 pound orecchiette
Sea salt and freshly ground black pepper
Parmigiano-Reggiano or Pecorino Romano cheese, grated

1. Steam the cauliflower for 10–15 minutes.

2. While the cauliflower is steaming, heat a large skillet and add 2 tablespoons of the olive oil. Sauté the onion in olive oil over moderate heat for 5–6 minutes. When translucent, add the garlic, sauté 1–2 minutes, and then add the tomatoes, white wine, and rosemary. Simmer uncovered over moderate heat for 10–12 minutes.

3. While sauce is cooking, in another skillet, heat the remaining 2 tablespoons of olive oil, and separately sauté the thinly sliced sausage rounds. When they are browned, add them to the tomato sauce, along with the cauliflower. Add additional broth or wine to the sauce until it is of a consistency where it will coat the back of a spoon.

4. Cook the orecchiette in a large pot of boiling water, to which you have added 1-2 tablespoons salt. Cook for 12 minutes (or according to package directions), reserve a cup of pasta water, and drain the orecchiette in a colander.

5. Put the orecchiette back in the pasta pot and add the sauce. Toss gently to incorporate the sauce, and thin with a few tablespoons of the reserved pasta water if it seems too thick. Taste carefully and add salt and pepper if you think it is needed. Serve with freshly grated Parmigiano-Reggiano or Pecorino Romano cheese.

Serves 6

Gnocchi with Fire Roasted Tomatoes, Sausage, and Cauliflower

I've recently discovered Original Field Roast Grain Meat Co., out of Seattle, Washington, and love its Italian Sausage with Eggplant, Fennel, Fresh Garlic, and Red Pepper. Unlike the Tofurky brand, the Field Roast sausages come in a casing that you need to cut away and discard. I also find that the Field Roast sausages crumble more easily and don't hold up well to frying. Consequently, I like to add them directly to my sauce, which cuts down on the amount of olive oil I use in preparing the dish. I like to use the Muir Glen Fire Roasted Diced Tomatoes instead of their regular diced tomatoes, because the fire roasting gives the sauce a lot more punch. Unlike the previous recipe, which uses orecchiette, this recipe uses whole wheat gnocchi or conchiglie (bite-sized shells). Real gnocchi are made with potatoes and are more like potato dumplings. This pasta shape is called gnocchi because it resembles the potato gnocchi you may have had in restaurants. If you can't find whole wheat gnocchi, whole wheat shells, or radiatori would be good, too.

1 head cauliflower, separated into florets
1 tablespoon extra virgin olive oil
½ onion, finely chopped
2 cloves garlic, minced or pressed
28-ounce can fire roasted diced tomatoes
¼ cup dry white wine
2 Field Roast Italian sausages, casings removed, quartered lengthwise, and then sliced in ¼-inch pieces
Sea salt and freshly ground black pepper
1 pound whole wheat gnocchi, shells, or radiatori
2-3 tablespoons minced Italian parsley
Parmigiano-Reggiano cheese, grated

1. Steam the cauliflower for 10–15 minutes.

2. While the cauliflower is steaming, heat a large skillet, add the olive oil, and gently sauté the onion 5–6 minutes until translucent. Add the garlic and gently sauté another 1–2 minutes. Add the tomatoes and white wine, and cook uncovered for about 10–12 minutes.

3. Add the sausage pieces and steamed cauliflower to the sauce and cook for 3–4 minutes. Taste and adjust seasoning with sea salt and freshly ground black pepper.

4. While you are making your sauce, cook the whole wheat gnocchi or shells in a large pot of boiling salted water for about 7–8 minutes (or according to package directions) until al dente. Reserve a cup of pasta water and drain the pasta into a colander.

5. Put the gnocchi back in the pasta pot and pour the sauce over the pasta. Thin with a few tablespoons of the reserved pasta water if it seems too thick and add the parsley. Serve with freshly grated Parmigiano-Reggiano cheese.

Serves 6

BAKED BELL PEPPERS STUFFED WITH SAUSAGE AND SPINACH

My childhood memory of stuffed bell peppers is that they were always rather bland affairs– white rice and ground beef, with not much else going for them. No wonder they weren't my favorite dinner! We get such lovely bell peppers almost year round in the Carolinas that I often buy more than I need at our local farmers' market. I bring home the red, yellow, and orange varieties for a fraction of the price charged in our local grocery stores, so I'm always looking for new things to do with them. I've used green bell peppers here, only because they are the least expensive variety—but if you find other varieties at a reasonable price, your plate will be more colorful and the dish will taste even better! I usually have an extra cup or so of leftover homemade tomato sauce in my fridge. If you don't, I've had good success with the bottled fire roasted tomato sauce made by any of the following companies: Muir Glen, Barilla, and Newman's Own.

3–4 ounces baby spinach, coarsely chopped
1 large egg
¼ cup milk
1 cup coarse bread crumbs (preferably from whole wheat bread), pulsed a few times in the food processor
½ cup freshly grated Parmigiano-Reggiano cheese (divided use)
2 tablespoons pine nuts
3 tablespoons extra virgin olive oil (divided use)
½ cup finely chopped red onion
2 Tofurky Italian sausages, sliced lengthwise into quarters and chopped into small pieces
2 large green bell peppers, halved lengthwise, cored, and seeded, with stems left intact
1–2 cups fire roasted tomato sauce

1. Preheat oven to 400°F.

2. Steam the spinach for 3–4 minutes. Put the spinach in a colander and let it cool. Press out all of the lovely green liquid from the steamed spinach, saving it for broth.

3. In a medium bowl, beat the egg and the milk. Mix in the coarse bread crumbs, ¼ cup of the grated Parmigiano-Reggiano cheese, and the pine nuts.

4. Heat a large skillet and add 1 tablespoon of olive oil. Sauté the onion for 5–6 minutes, and then add the sausage pieces. Sauté for another 3–4 minutes. Let cool.

5. Add the cooled onion, sausage, and well-drained spinach to the bowl. Adjust seasonings if needed with sea salt and freshly ground black pepper.

6. Sauté the pepper halves in about 2 tablespoons of olive oil on both sides, just to soften them a little. (When I've been short on time, I have omitted sautéing the pepper halves and still had good results.) Pack the stuffing mixture into the pepper halves.

7. Pour the tomato sauce into a lightly greased baking dish. Add the stuffed peppers, filling side up. Sprinkle with the remaining ¼ cup of grated Parmigiano-Reggiano. Cover the baking dish with aluminum foil and bake for 30 minutes. Remove the aluminum foil and continue baking for 5-10 minutes more.

Serves 4

ITALIAN SAUSAGE WITH FENNEL AND OLIVES

By now, you know that I love fennel, because I use it in so many of my recipes. If you aren't familiar with fennel, please give it a try. It's readily available in our farmers' market, even in the winter months, where I can often buy a large bulb for a buck. Fennel looks a little like celery, with a large bulb at the bottom of the stalk, but it is really a member of the parsley family. Its Italian name is finocchio, and it smells a little like licorice. It is crisp, sweet, and delicious, either raw in salads or cooked. Although I often pair it with tomatoes, this recipe uses onion, garlic, black and green olives, and two different brands of sausage. This preparation uses a lot of sausage, which emphasizes the sausage instead of the vegetables. I use two kinds of sausage because my son and I prefer the Tofurky Italian sausages, but my husband also likes the Lightlife brand. I've recently become enamored with Field Roast Italian sausage, which also works very well in this recipe. If you use the Field Roast and the Tofurky brands and leave out the cheese, this recipe can be vegan. On the other hand, if you want to simplify your life, you can simply use two packages of whatever meat analogue sausage brand your family prefers.

3 tablespoons extra virgin olive oil (divided use)
1 onion, finely chopped
4 cloves garlic, peeled and left whole
1 teaspoon crushed red pepper flakes
2 fennel bulbs, quartered lengthwise, bottoms, tops and core removed, and thinly sliced
1 cup vegetable stock (divided use)
1 cup white wine (divided use)
⅔ cup Calamata olives, pitted and sliced
⅓ cup green olives, pitted and sliced
4 Tofurky Italian sausages (1 package)
4 Lightlife Italian sausages (1 package) or 4 Field Roast Italian sausages (1 package), casings removed
Sea salt and freshly ground black pepper
Freshly grated Parmigiano-Reggiano (optional)

1. Heat a skillet and add 2 tablespoons of olive oil. Sauté the onion over moderate heat for 5–6 minutes until the onion is translucent. Add the whole garlic cloves and sauté for another minute.

2. Add the crushed red pepper and sliced fennel and sauté for another 3–4 minutes. Season with salt and pepper, ½ cup of the stock, and ½ cup of the wine. Cover and cook for about 8 minutes. Add the olives, and cook for 10–12 more minutes until the fennel is very tender.

3. While the fennel is cooking, heat the remaining tablespoon of olive oil in another large skillet, and cook the whole sausages until lightly browned, about 4 minutes. Add the remaining wine and stock and simmer for about 5–6 minutes. Take off the heat.

4. Cut each sausage in half and add to the fennel mixture. Cook uncovered for about 5 more minutes. Remove the whole garlic cloves if they offend you, or leave them in—your choice. Taste carefully, and add a little sea salt and freshly ground black pepper.

5. Serve immediately with the optional grated Parmigiano-Reggiano.

Serves 6–8

CONCHIGLIE WITH CREAMY TOMATO AND SAUSAGE SAUCE

Conchiglie is the Italian word for "shells," a pasta shape that comes in many different sizes. From the tiny conchigliette or lumanchine, which are wonderful in my Spanish Garbanzo Chipotle Soup and my Baked Stuffed Shells with Fire Roasted Sausage Sauce, which immediately follows this recipe, I think shells should be a staple in any well stocked pantry. Don't worry, though, if your pantry lacks shells tonight. This sauce will still be very good with farfalle or cavatappi. I'd actually forgotten how tasty this dish is – and how simple it is to prepare – until I re-discovered it again in my notes from 2008. Remember, easy weeknight meals don't have to be just single note meals. Use your time wisely. While your sauce is cooking, prep some asparagus, broccoli, green beans or zucchini for the steamer, or make a green leafy salad. Only you know what you have in the fridge that may be past its prime in the next day or two.

2 tablespoons unsalted butter
2 Field Roast Italian sausages, casing removed and sliced into ¼ inch pieces
28-ounce can diced tomatoes, drained (with juice reserved)
1 sprig fresh rosemary
1–2 bay leaves
Generous sprinkling of red pepper flakes
⅔ cup heavy cream
2 tablespoons Italian parsley, minced
Sea salt and freshly ground black pepper
1 pound conchiglie (medium-sized shells), farfalle, or cavatappi
Freshly grated Parmigiano-Reggiano cheese

1. Melt the butter in a large sauce pan or skillet, and sauté the sausage pieces for about 3–4 minutes. Be careful, because the Field Roast sausages can crumble easily. Remove the sausage pieces from the pan, and set aside.

2. In the same pan, add the drained tomatoes, reserving the juice in case you need to thin the sauce a bit later.

3. Add the whole sprig of rosemary, bay leaves and red pepper. Cook for about 10–12 minutes until the sauce starts to thicken. Remove the rosemary sprig and the bay leaves.

4. Pour in the cream and cook until the sauce reduces and can coat the back of a spoon. Add the parsley, black pepper, sea salt, and reserved sausage. Remove the rosemary sprig and the bay leaves. Keep the sauce warm over very low heat while you cook your pasta.

5. When your pasta is cooked al dente, reserve a cup of the pasta cooking water. Drain the pasta and add it to the skillet, along with the grated cheese. If the sauce seems a bit thick, add a few tablespoons of the reserved pasta cooking water to loosen the sauce. Adjust the seasonings and serve with additional grated cheese.

Serves 4–6

BAKED STUFFED SHELLS WITH FIRE ROASTED SAUSAGE SAUCE

I adore no-boil lasagna noodles and often wondered whether the same techniques would work with other kinds of stuffed pastas that aren't similarly labeled. Stuffed shells are a favorite dish that I rarely make because of the hassle of boiling the shells. Some of the shells tear and stuffing the floppy shells with my ricotta mixture requires more dexterity than I can muster. I've tested this recipe several times and found that it was easy to stuff the uncooked shells and the large quantity of hot sauce cooked the shells to perfection in an hour. The sauce for this recipe is rich with slow-cooked vegetables, with a little less emphasis on the sausage than in some of my other sauces. To make stuffing the shells easy, simply spoon the ricotta mixture into a plastic sandwich bag. Squeeze out the air, cut the tip off one corner of the bag, and use your improvised pastry bag to fill the shells. I specify 20 ounces of ricotta (about 2½ cups), because when I only use a 16-ounce container, I sometimes have shells left over and not enough filling.

2 tablespoons extra virgin olive oil
1 large onion, finely chopped
1 stalk celery, diced
2 carrots, diced
3 cloves garlic, pressed or minced
5–6 crimini mushrooms, cleaned and sliced
28-ounce can fire roasted crushed tomatoes
28-ounce can petite diced tomatoes
2 bay leaves
3 sprigs Italian parsley
2 sprigs of basil
3 sprigs of oregano
4–5 sprigs of thyme
Sea salt and coarsely ground black pepper
3 small zucchini, diced
¼ cup white wine (optional)
2 Field Roast Italian Sausages, cut or crumbled into small pieces
20 ounces ricotta cheese
1 egg
1 cup grated Parmigiano-Reggiano (divided use)
½ cup grated mozzarella
½ cup grated Pecorino Romano
Several grinds of nutmeg
3–4 sprigs Italian parsley, finely minced
Sea salt and freshly ground black pepper
16-ounce box jumbo shells (conchiglie giganti)
½ pound mozzarella, grated

1. Heat a large skillet, add the olive oil, and sauté the onion for 5–6 minutes until translucent. Add the celery and carrots and sauté for 5 more minutes. Add the garlic and mushrooms, and continue to sauté for 5 more minutes. While your vegetables are sautéing, put a liner in your slow cooker, open the cans of tomatoes and dump them in. You can also get your herbs and dice your zucchini. When the sautéed vegetables are cooked, add them to the slow cooker along with the herbs, diced zucchini, and the optional wine. Set the slow cooker on high, cover it, and cook for 4–5 hours. (Or if you need to be away from home longer, set it on simmer and cook everything for 7–8 hours.)

2. About 2 hours before you want to eat, chop the sausage into small pieces and add it to the sauce. Begin making the ricotta mixture for stuffing the shells. In a medium sized mixing bowl, break an egg and beat it with a whisk. Add the ricotta, mozzarella, ½ cup of grated Parmigiano-Reggiano, Pecorino Romano, nutmeg, parsley, and freshly ground black pepper, and mix thoroughly. Put the mixture in a plastic sandwich bag, squeeze out the air, and cut off the tip of one corner of the bag.

3. Preheat your oven to 350°F. Lightly oil a large baking dish or spray with non-stick cooking spray. Put a layer of cooked sauce on the bottom. Assuming you're right handed, take a shell in your left hand and squeeze some of the ricotta filling into the space inside the shell. (You'll find that each shell looks different – some are more open and others are tightly closed. I'd suggest using the more open ones for the first time you make this dish because they will be the easiest to neatly stuff with the ricotta mixture.) Fill all the shells with the ricotta mixture and place them in the pan.

4. Return to the sauce and take out the bay leaves and the herb sprigs. Taste the sauce and adjust for seasonings, adding a little additional sea salt and freshly ground pepper if needed. Pour all of the sauce over the stuffed shells. Cover with aluminum foil and bake for 60 minutes. Uncover and test the shells to make sure that they pierce easily with a knife. If they don't, cover the shells again with the aluminum foil, and cook for another 10 minutes.

5. Put the last ingredient, the grated mozzarella, on top of the stuffed shells and return the uncovered pan to the oven for 10–15 minutes. When you take it out of the oven, sprinkle the remaining ½ cup grated Parmigiano-Reggiano on top. Let the shells cool slightly before serving.

Serves 6–8

RISOTTO WITH SPINACH, PEPPERS, AND SAUSAGE

Risotto is a classic recipe that's a favorite in my family. Instead of the green peas that are often used in many risotto recipes, I use sliced ribbons of fresh baby spinach. I also use two different colors of peppers for contrast and cut the sausages into very small pieces after lightly grilling them so they incorporate well into the risotto. We were delighted with the depth of flavor. We enjoyed this with a Cupcake Sauvignon Blanc, which provided the dry white wine needed for the recipe. A Pinot Noir would have been equally good, but it wouldn't have served double duty as the wine to make the risotto. If you prefer to serve this dish with a Pinot Noir, use dry vermouth instead of wine.

2 tablespoons extra virgin olive oil (divided use)
2 Tofurky Italian sausages
4–6 cups vegetable stock
1 onion, finely chopped
3 cloves garlic, pressed
1 cup mixed red, yellow, green, or orange bell peppers, chopped
2 cups Arborio rice
½ cup dry white wine or vermouth
2–3 ounces baby spinach, finely sliced into thin ribbons (about 2–3 cups)
¾ cup grated Parmigiano-Reggiano cheese (plus extra for the table)
Sea salt and freshly ground black pepper

1. In large skillet, heat a tablespoon of olive oil. When the skillet is hot, cook the sausages for a couple of minutes until lightly browned, turning them every 30–45 seconds. Remove the sausages from the skillet and set aside on paper towels until cool. When cool, quarter each sausage lengthwise, and slice into ¼-inch pieces.

2. Heat the broth or stock in a medium sauce pan over low heat.

3. Add remaining tablespoon of olive oil to the skillet in which you sautéed the sausage. Add the onion and cook for 5–6 minutes over moderate heat. Add the garlic, and cook for another minute. Add the bell pepper pieces and sauté for 5 more minutes. Add the rice, and sauté for a minute or two before adding the white wine or vermouth. Sauté until the rice has completely absorbed the wine, about 3–4 minutes. Begin adding broth or stock, about ½ cup at a time, and cook until liquid is absorbed. Keep stirring the risotto and adding liquid until the rice is just barely al dente.

4. When the rice is al dente, add the spinach. Cover the skillet and turn the heat to low for two minutes. Uncover and add the sausage pieces. Cook and stir for a minute. Stir in cheese and a little sea salt and pepper to taste. Cover and let stand 2 minutes. Stir again, adjust the seasonings and serve immediately.

Serves 4–6

Torchiette with Broccoli, Sausage, and Roasted Tomatoes

I created this dish for my fifty-seventh birthday party—an Italian wine tasting at Total Wine that I "won" in a charity silent auction. Amy, the fabulous wine team consultant who did our tasting, worked with me on the best pairing of food and wine after I told her what I planned to make. Eight courses in just under two hours—and each one was better than the one before it! Here was my accompaniment to an unbelievably good Vasco Sassetti Brunello 2004. The torchiette was served at room temperature, but if you can eat it hot, it's even more tasty. You may not be familiar with torchiette, but it means "little torches." It is a lovely twisted pasta that catches sauce beautifully and is a pleasure to eat. If you can't find torchiette, cavatappi, fusilli, or farfalle would also work well.

1 pint cherry tomatoes, sliced in half, pole to pole
4–5 garlic cloves, peeled but left whole
Extra virgin olive oil
1 pound broccoli cut in very small florets, with stems reserved
1 Baby Vidalia onion, finely minced
2 gloves garlic, pressed
2 Field Roast Italian sausages, quartered lengthwise and cut into very small pieces
¼ cup white wine
1 pound torchiette, cavatappi, fusilli, or farfalle
Pecorino Romano cheese, grated
Freshly ground black pepper and sea salt
½ lemon, juiced, optional

1. Preheat oven to 400°F. Line a rimmed baking sheet with non-stick foil. Toss the sliced cherry tomatoes and whole garlic cloves with a couple of tablespoons of olive oil and roast them in the oven for about 25 minutes. Remove from the oven and cool on a rack. Turn off the oven.

2. As the tomatoes are roasting, prep the broccoli. Put a large pot of water on to boil for the pasta. Once it is boiling, add 2 teaspoons of salt and any portion of the broccoli stems that you're not using in this dish. The broccoli stems will help to flavor the water, so just let them boil while you finish up your prep work.

3. Steam the broccoli over the boiling pot of water or in a steamer for 6–8 minutes. Remove to a colander in the sink, and add some ice to stop cooking and preserve the broccoli's fresh green color.

4. Heat a large skillet and add 1–2 tablespoons of olive oil. Sauté the onion for 5–6 minutes, followed by the garlic for a minute. Add the sausage pieces and cook for 2–3 minutes before you add the wine. When the wine is absorbed, turn off the heat, and cover the pan.

5. Add the cooked broccoli to the sausage and onion mixture, and put the torchiette into the pot of boiling pasta water. Cook the torchiette for the lowest amount of time specified on the package.

6. Once the torchiette is al dente, reserve about a cup of pasta water, and then drain the pasta in a colander.

7. Toss the pasta with the sausage, onion and broccoli mixture, the roasted tomatoes, and the garlic. Add a few tablespoons of the pasta water if the sauce needs thinning.

8. Toss in about a cup of grated Pecorino Romano. Taste and correct seasonings, adding a bit of sea salt and freshly ground black pepper. If you are serving this dish at room temperature, add the lemon juice and a little more olive oil.

9. Top with grated Pecorino Romano.

Serves 6–8 as a main course (or 15–20 in smaller portions)

JAMBALAYA

On the Tuesday before Lent begins, we celebrate Mardi Gras in our home. We don beads, wear purple, green and gold, play some jazz, and pretend we're in New Orleans! I generally make jambalaya at Mardi Gras because good, fresh okra is hard to get in late winter in the Carolinas. Since a Cajun Jambalaya never uses tomatoes, this is actually more of a Creole Jambalaya. I like to use fire roasted diced tomatoes because they give the dish a bit more of a smoky flavor. I also take a great deal of liberty by calling this "jambalaya" because I cook my rice separately. Classic jambalaya is bit more like paella because the rice is added directly to the pot of stewing stock, vegetables, and meats. This cooking technique allows the rice to absorb flavor while it cooks. However, we prefer brown rice to white rice in our home. Since brown rice takes much longer to cook than white rice, I have not yet figured out the perfect timing of when to add brown rice to the pot—although I'm still working on it! My current version of jambalaya might not fool a New Orleans native, but it may well fool your family carnivores. Try serving it with mashed sweet potatoes and a nice Rioja. A Spanish Rioja we particularly like is the 2009 Barón de Barbón Tempranillo Rioja.

2 tablespoons extra virgin olive oil
1–1½ cups onions, finely chopped
2 celery stalks, sliced lengthwise in halves or thirds, and then finely chopped in ¼-inch pieces
1 cup green bell pepper, diced
2 bay leaves
4 garlic cloves
⅓ cup vegetable stock
28-ounce can fire roasted diced tomatoes
4 sprigs thyme
1 teaspoon hot pepper flakes
1 teaspoon Old Bay seasoning
2 Field Roast Mexican Chipotle Sausages (½ package), casings removed
2 Field Roast Italian Sausages (½ package), casings removed
8-ounce package of WestSoy Seitan Strips
½ cup dry white wine or vermouth
Sea salt and freshly ground black pepper
1 teaspoon gumbo filé powder (optional)[26]
1½ cups brown rice, cooked for about 55 minutes

---

26 Gumbo filé powder is made from dried sassafras leaves. I found a version made by Zatarain's in the spice section of my local grocery store. If you have trouble finding it, it's also available on the Internet from Williams Sonoma, Amazon, and a host of other purveyors. A small jar will last you a long time. Don't despair if you can't find it—your jambalaya will still be very good without it.

1. Heat a skillet, and add the olive oil. Add the onions and cook for about 6–7 minutes over medium heat.

2. Add the celery and green bell peppers and cook for about 4–5 minutes. Turn down the heat a bit, and add the garlic and bay leaves and cook a minute or so more. Add the stock and cook for another 5 minutes.

3. Put a liner in your slow cooker, and add the sautéed vegetables, tomatoes, thyme, hot pepper flakes, and Old Bay. Set the slow cooker on simmer and cover it while you prepare the sausages.

4. After removing the casings, slice each sausage lengthwise in half, and then in half again, so you have four long strips. Slice the strips into ½-inch pieces.

5. Add the sausages to the empty skillet, and sauté for 3–5 minutes until just beginning to brown. Put the sausage pieces in the slow cooker.

6. Depending on their size, you may have to cut some of the seitan strips into slightly smaller pieces. I love their irregular shape, but you may want them smaller. Using the same skillet, sauté the seitan strips for just a minute or so and add to the slow cooker.

7. Return the skillet to the burner and add the white wine. Deglaze the pan over medium heat and scrape in all the little scraps of sausage and seitan. Add the contents of the skillet to the slow cooker. Cover and cook on high for 4 hours or simmer for about 6 hours.

8. Taste carefully and correct seasonings with sea salt and pepper. Add the gumbo filé powder if you're using it and let it cook on warm for a few minutes. Don't cook gumbo filé powder over direct heat or it will get stringy instead of thickening your sauce. Serve over brown rice.

Serves 6–8

Brazilian Feijoada

Feijoada has been a staple in my culinary repertoire ever since I was introduced to the dish by Frances Moore Lappé in her seminal book, *Diet for a Small Planet*.[27] It seemed exotic to me as a teen, and the hearty flavor of the beans was very satisfying on a brisk autumn evening. I've made many versions of feijoada in my life, and this one owes a thankful nod to Crescent Dragonwagon and Molly Katzen. The traditional version uses a lot of meat—sausage, pork, bacon, and beef. My menfolk think that I get a good flavor using a mixture of chorizo and Italian sausage.

3 cans[28] black beans
2 tablespoons extra virgin olive oil
1 onion, chopped
2 cloves garlic, minced or pressed
1 stalk celery, chopped
1 red bell pepper, chopped
½ teaspoon ground cumin
2 bay leaves
Sea salt and freshly ground black pepper
½ cup chopped fresh tomatoes (try quartered grape tomatoes since they hold their shape well)
½ cup vegetarian stock or broth
2 oranges, zested and juiced
1 orange, peeled, sectioned and chopped
1 lime, juiced
¼ cup red wine
2 Trader Joe's Soy Chorizo sausages (1 package) or 2 Field Roast Mexican Chipotle Sausages (½ package)
2 Field Roast Italian Sausages (½ package)
1–2 tablespoons apple cider vinegar
½–1 teaspoon hot pepper sauce
Cooked brown rice

1. Put a liner in the slow cooker and turn to high. Drain and rinse 2 cans of black beans, and add them to the slow cooker, along with the remaining can of un-rinsed black beans.

---

27 Frances Moore Lappé, *Diet for a Small Planet* (New York: Ballantine Books, 1973), 134–136.
28 Cans of beans vary in size, depending on the brand. In my pantry I have 15-ounce cans, 15.5-ounce cans, 16-ounce cans, and 19-ounce cans of black beans. The difference is so small that it won't matter which size you use in this recipe.

2. Heat a skillet, add the olive oil, and sauté the onion for 7-8 minutes over low heat. When the onion is translucent, add the garlic, and then the celery. Sauté for about 5 minutes and add the red pepper, cumin, bay leaves, salt and pepper. Sauté a few more minutes and then add to the slow cooker.

3. Add the chopped tomatoes, stock, orange zest, orange juice, sectioned orange, lime juice, and red wine. Cook on high for 5 hours.

4. About 30 minutes before you are ready to serve, cook the sausages, lightly sautéing in a little olive oil for about 4–5 minutes. (If you are using Trader Joe's instead of Field Roast, it will crumble very easily when you take it out of the casing, so you may just want to lightly sauté the crumbled pieces and not try to keep it whole.) Let cool, quarter each sausage lengthwise, and chop into small pieces. Add the chopped sausage pieces to the slow cooker and cook for about 10-15 minutes. Add the vinegar and hot pepper sauce right before serving over plenty of cooked brown rice.

Serves 6–8

Chorizo Pasta with Tomatoes, Spinach, and Mozzarella

This recipe *is* a tad spicy. But it's very good, and so easy to make. I love the taste of fresh mozzarella, but when you cut it up, it often gets stringy. If you buy the tiny perlini or perline[29] mozzarella balls, they will soften in the sauce, but still stay intact. Instead of Parmigiano-Reggiano or Pecorino Romano, I've suggested grated Asiago in this recipe. It's still a grana type cheese, but a lot less costly. It's also milder and less nutty, which I think complements the spiciness of the chorizo perfectly. My husband said this was incredibly delectable!

1 pound mini farfalle
1–2 tablespoons salt
2 tablespoons extra virgin olive oil
12-ounce package Lightlife Smart Sausages Chorizo Style, quartered lengthwise, and chopped into ½-inch pieces
3 cloves garlic, pressed or minced
1 to 1½ cups diced fresh tomatoes
½ cup vegetable stock or broth
½ cup fire roasted tomato juice or V8 Spicy Hot Vegetable Juice
3–4 sprigs fresh oregano
4 ounce baby spinach, thinly sliced
8 ounces perlini or perline mozzarella balls (see footnote)
4–6 leaves fresh basil, minced
Sea salt and freshly ground black pepper
Hot pepper sauce (optional)
Asiago cheese, grated

1. Bring a large pot of water to a boil for your pasta and add 1-2 tablespoons salt.

2. Sauté the chorizo in olive oil for a minute or so. Add the garlic and cook for 1 minute. Add the tomatoes, stock, fire roasted tomato juice, oregano sprigs, and slivered spinach to the chorizo mixture.

3. Cover and cook for 15–18 minutes over moderate heat. Remove the sprigs of oregano.

4. Put the pasta in the pot of boiling water and cook according to package directions.

---

29   Perline or perlini are very tiny mozzarella balls, usually packaged in water. The brand I use is Palazzina Mozzarella, Perline style. They are fairly perishable, so use them quickly after opening the package.

5. When the pasta is ready, drain it in a colander and add to the chorizo tomato mixture. Take it off the heat. Add the mozzarella balls and basil, toss gently to incorporate, and cover for 2 minutes.

6. Adjust seasonings. Serve with grated Asiago.

Serves 6

CLASSIC RED BEANS AND RICE WITH CHORIZO

This is a hearty dish that cries out for a great red wine. Consider opening a rich Malbec or a Cabernet Sauvignon. No wimpy red wines for this dish! The beans will cook all day in your slow cooker, and their aroma will permeate your home. I normally don't add salt to my bean-soaking water, but brining the red beans worked well for me in this recipe and didn't seem to toughen the skins. You'll have about twenty minutes of work to do when you get home and then the stew will need to cook for another hour, so don't make this on a day when you need to eat the minute you walk in the door.

1 pound red beans
1 tablespoon salt
2 bay leaves
2 cloves garlic, finely sliced or pressed
3 tablespoon extra virgin olive oil (divided use)
1 large onion, finely chopped
1 large red bell pepper, chopped into small pieces
1 package Trader Joe's Soy Chorizo (2 sausages), casings removed, halved lengthwise, and chopped into ¼-inch pieces
3 MorningStar Farms Veggie Bacon Strips, chopped in ¼-inch pieces
Sea salt and freshly ground black pepper
Brown rice, boiled or steamed in a rice cooker
1 avocado, diced
1 lime, juiced

1. Soak beans overnight in about 8 cups of water and 1 tablespoon sea salt.

2. In the morning, drain the beans and rinse with fresh water.

3. Line your slow cooker with a liner, and add the soaked beans and 4–6 cups of water. Add the bay leaves and garlic, and cook on high for 8 hours.

4. When you get home from work, heat 1½ tablespoons olive oil in a skillet and sauté the onion for about 5-6 minutes. When it is translucent, add the red bell pepper, sauté for about 3–4 minutes, and then add the skillet contents to the slow cooker.

5. Sauté the chorizo in 1½ tablespoons olive oil for 4–5 minutes and remove from skillet.

6. In the same skillet you used to cook the chorizo, sauté the bacon strips briefly, and then add them and the chorizo to the slow cooker. Cook on high for at least another hour while you make your brown rice.

7. About 5 minutes before serving, dice the avocado, and douse with lime juice and a little sea salt.

8. When the rice is done, put it around the edge of a pretty soup bowl and put the red beans and chorizo in the center. Top with the diced avocado.

Serves 6–8

Tomato, Corn, and Chorizo Stew

This is a super easy supper—perfect for a weeknight in late summer when corn is still at its peak. Although couscous is sometimes thought of as a grain, it is actually a tiny pasta made from semolina. We buy the whole wheat couscous which only takes five to eight minutes to cook. It is perfect for weeknights when time is at a premium.

2 tablespoons extra virgin olive oil
1 onion, chopped
1 clove garlic, minced
1 red bell pepper, chopped
3 ears fresh sweet corn
12-ounce package Trader Joe's Soy Chorizo, casing removed, cut or crumbled into small pieces (2 sausages)
28-ounce can of diced fire roasted tomatoes
1 large tomato, chopped
2 tablespoons brown sugar
1–2 teaspoons Zatarain seasoning
1 bay leaf
Sea salt and freshly ground black pepper
1¼ cups water
1 teaspoon unsalted butter
¼ teaspoon sea salt
1 cup whole wheat couscous

1. Heat a large skillet and add the olive oil. Sauté the onion for 5–6 minutes until translucent. Lower the heat and add the garlic and pepper. Cook for 5–6 minutes. While the onions, garlic and pepper are cooking, microwave the corn in its husks for about 10 minutes. (If you prefer to not use a microwave, remove the husks and steam or boil the corn.)

2. Add the chorizo to the skillet and sauté for another 2-3 minutes.

3. Take the corn out of the microwave, shuck it, and rinse under running water to make sure that there are no strings left from the husks. Cut the corn off the cob and add it to the sauté.

4. Next add the chopped tomato, fire roasted tomatoes, brown sugar, Zatarain, bay leaf, salt, and pepper and simmer for 10–15 minutes.

5. While the stew is simmering, boil the water in a small sauce pan, along with the optional salt and butter. When the water boils, add the couscous, stir it quickly, cover tightly, and turn off the heat. Let it stand for 5–6 minutes. Uncover and fluff with a fork.

6. Adjust the seasoning of the stew. Serve with the couscous and garlic bread or French bread, warmed in the oven.

Serves 4

CANNELLINI CHORIZO STEW

This recipe will take you about fifteen minutes to prepare and assemble before you leave for work. Your efforts will be rewarded when you walk in the door knowing that all you have to do is wash and slice the spinach, sauté the sausages, make a salad, and dinner will be on the table. You can use your own homemade beans, if you were smart enough to soak dried cannellini beans overnight and then cook them for about ten minutes in the pressure cooker while sautéing the onion, garlic, carrots and celery in the morning. Unfortunately, I'm normally not that well organized. Consequently, I suggest using canned Progresso cannellini beans, which I think are almost as good as the dried ones I make and pressure cook. Please note that Progresso cannellini beans come in a nineteen-ounce can, so if you use another brand in the industry standard fifteen-ounce can, you will have a little less soup than if you use Progresso cannellini beans. Serve the stew in deep soup bowls with freshly grated Parmigiano-Reggiano and finely chopped Italian parsley. A big green salad, a crusty baguette or rosemary olive oil bread, and a fine Rioja will round out this meal.

2 tablespoons extra virgin olive oil (divided use)
1 onion, chopped
2 cloves garlic, chopped
2 carrots, diced
1 or 2 celery stalks, diced
2 tomatoes, roughly chopped (about 1 cup)
1 large or 2 medium potatoes, peeled and cubed
1 teaspoon paprika
3 cups vegetable stock
2 tablespoons tomato paste
2 19-ounce cans cannellini beans, drained and rinsed
1 bunch spinach, washed well and sliced into thin ribbons
4 Lightlife Smart Sausages Chorizo Style
Freshly grated Parmigiano-Reggiano
3–4 tablespoons finely chopped parsley

1. Heat a skillet and add 1 tablespoon olive oil. Sauté the onion for 5–6 minutes until translucent. Add the diced carrots and celery, and sauté about 4–5 minutes more. Add the garlic and sauté for one more minute.

2. Prep the tomatoes and potatoes, and assemble the other ingredients while the vegetables are sautéing.

3. Put a liner in the slow cooker. Add the contents of the skillet, the tomatoes and potatoes, paprika, stock, tomato paste, and cannellini beans. Stir a bit to make sure everything is well mixed. Cover the slow cooker and cook 4–5 hours on high or up to 8 hours on low.

4. When you get home, check the slow cooker. If it has cycled down to the warm setting, turn it back up to high. Wash the spinach well and slice it into thin ribbons. Add the spinach ribbons to the slow cooker. Lightly sauté the chorizo sausages in the remaining tablespoon of olive oil. Let cool slightly. Quarter the sausages lengthwise, thinly slice, and add the sausage pieces to the slow cooker. Cook for about 10 minutes while you make the salad. Serve in deep soup bowls with some crusty bread.

Serves 6

Spanish Garbanzo Chipotle Soup

This is another easy recipe to make in the slow cooker before you leave for work. It's simple, filling, and very satisfying on a cold day. This may sound silly, but I actually like canned garbanzo beans better than the real thing made from dried beans. Maybe I've worked with "old" dried garbanzo beans too many times, but my garbanzos never seem to cook up soft enough for my family's taste—even after soaking them overnight and cooking them in the pressure cooker. As a result, I usually used canned garbanzos and Progresso has become my favorite brand. Please note that Progresso garbanzos come in a nineteen-ounce can, so if you use another brand in the industry standard fifteen-ounce can, you will have a little less soup than if you use Progresso garbanzo beans. I also like the flavor of the liquid that comes with the Progresso garbanzos, so I add the liquid instead of draining and rinsing the beans as I normally do. I like to dice the onion, celery, carrots, and green bell pepper into quarter-inch pieces, and chop the new potatoes into slightly larger half-inch pieces so that they will hold their shape in the soup. I use red-skin new potatoes for color, and just scrub them well, without peeling them. Add the sausage on the top of each bowl of soup, so that you can add as much or as little as each family member likes. The Field Roast Mexican Chipotle sausage is very spicy—so I give my husband a lot more of the sausage than I serve myself. Sop up the delicious soup with a crusty bread like sesame semolina.

2 tablespoons extra virgin olive oil (divided use)
½ cup onion, diced in ¼-inch pieces
½ cup celery, diced in ¼-inch pieces
½ cup carrots, diced in ¼-inch pieces
½ cup green bell pepper, diced in ¼-inch pieces
3 cloves garlic, pressed
2 19-ounce cans garbanzo beans (see head note)
8-10 small red skin potatoes, scrubbed well and chopped in ½-inch pieces (about 2 cups)
1 bay leaf
1 cup vegetable stock
2 Field Roast Mexican Chipotle sausages, casings removed, quartered lengthwise, and then cut into small pieces
¼ cup vegetable stock

1. Heat the skillet and add 1 tablespoon olive oil when the skillet is hot. Sauté the diced onion over medium heat for about 5–6 minutes, and then add the diced celery, carrot, and green bell pepper and cook for another 5–6 minutes. When all of the vegetables are softened and just starting to color, add the garlic and cook for just a minute so that it doesn't burn.

2. Put a liner in the slow cooker and add the sautéed veggies, along with the beans, potatoes, bay leaf, and the stock. Cover the slow cooker and cook at least 4–5 hours on high or up to 8 hours on low. Remove the bay leaf.

3. Heat 1 tablespoon olive oil in the same skillet you used for the veggies, and lightly sauté the sausage pieces. Add ¼ cup stock and let cook for about 3 minutes until the stock is almost gone. Top each bowl of soup with some of the sausage.

Serves 4-5

Meltingly Tender Beer Brats with Cabbage and Spuds

This version, simmered in the slow cooker and then finished in the oven, is similar to a few of my other recipes, but I think that the time in the oven (and the addition of the grated Gouda) makes it special. Serve it with buttered no-yolk egg noodles, sprinkled with poppy seeds, and some pumpernickel bread.

½ cup apple cider vinegar
½ cup white wine
⅓ cup brown sugar
1 teaspoon dried dill or 2 tablespoons fresh dill, minced
Sea salt and freshly ground black pepper
1 small green cabbage, quartered, cored and sliced thinly or chopped
½ red onion, finely chopped
4 Tofurky Beer Brats, left whole (14-ounce package)
4 large russet potatoes, cut in ½-inch slices
1 cup vegetable stock or broth
2 tablespoons unsalted butter
2 tablespoons flour
5–6 ounces Gouda cheese, grated

1. Mix the apple cider vinegar, wine, brown sugar, dill, salt, and pepper in a small bowl.

2. Put a liner in the slow cooker. Place the sliced cabbage and onion on the bottom, followed by the beer brats. Pour on the liquid mixture from step 1 and then layer the sliced potatoes. Pour the stock over the spuds, and add a little more salt and pepper. Cover the slow cooker and cook on low for 6–8 hours.

3. Lightly coat a large baking dish with cooking spray. Preheat oven to 400°F.

4. Remove the layer of potatoes and set aside. Put all of the cabbage, onion, and brat mixture in the baking dish. Pour the cooking liquid from the slow cooker into a liquid measuring cup or a bowl. You will need at least a cup of cooking liquid. If you don't have enough, add some stock or broth.

5. Put the potatoes back on top of the cabbage, onion, and brat mixture.

6. Melt the butter in a small sauce pan. Stir in the flour to make a roux[30] and cook for about 2 minutes. Slowly stir in the still-warm cooking liquid and cook over low heat, stirring frequently to make a medium-thick sauce. Adjust the seasonings to taste and pour the sauce over the potatoes.

7. Sprinkle with cheese and pop in the oven for 15–20 minutes, while you make the buttered poppy seed noodles.

Serves 4

---

30   A roux is the basis for many classic sauces. A roux thickens your sauce and is made by simply cooking equal amounts of flour and butter for a few minutes over low heat to eliminate any raw flour taste. The roux is now ready for you to add a warm liquid to it—in this case, stock or broth.

Easy Skillet Bratwurst Dinner

Some winter nights, when I haven't been well organized enough to set up my slow cooker in the morning, it's nice to be able to get dinner on the table in less than 30 minutes. The beauty of meat analogue sausage is that it cooks so quickly. Seeded rye bread would be a great accompaniment to this simple, hearty dish.

1 tablespoon extra virgin olive oil
1 leek or small onion, sliced thinly
2 tablespoons unsalted butter
4 russet potatoes, diced into ¼-inch pieces
1 red bell pepper, diced into ¼-inch pieces
½ cup dry white wine
¼–½ cup vegetable broth or stock
1 teaspoon caraway seeds
1 teaspoon dried dill weed or 2 tablespoons minced fresh dill leaves
Sea salt and freshly ground black pepper
4 Tofurky Beer Brats, thinly sliced (14-ounce package)
1½ cups grated Jarlsburg cheese
½–¾ cup grated Havarti cheese

1. Heat a skillet and add the olive oil. Sauté the leek or onion 5–6 minutes over moderate heat until translucent.

2. Add unsalted butter to the skillet. Once it's melted, add the diced potatoes and sauté 5–7 minutes.

3. Add red bell pepper. Sauté for 2–3 minutes, and add the wine and broth or stock. Stir well, cover and cook for 8–10 minutes.

4. Add caraway seeds, dill, sea salt, pepper, and the beer brats. Cover and cook for 5 minutes.

5. Add the grated cheeses. Lower the heat, cover the skillet, and cook for 2 minutes.

Serves 4

FRENCH ONION BRATS

If you have some leftover homemade French Onion Soup (please consult the index for my recipe), this dish is a snap to make. If you don't have leftover soup and still want to try it, substitute a can of Wolfgang Puck French Onion Soup, which is vegetarian-based and fairly low in sodium. If you use another brand, please check the label because most are made with beef broth and are very high in sodium. Please read the recipe carefully, because there are important differences depending on whether you've used the homemade soup or the canned soup. You will not need the additional butter or flour if you are using homemade soup because you will stop at step 4. This is a delicious winter meal with a Côtes du Rhône and a crusty baguette to sop up the sauce.

6 potatoes, peeled and sliced into ¼-inch slices
Mrs. Dash garlic-onion blend
½ pound carrots, peeled and sliced on the diagonal in ½-inch slices
14-ounce package Tofurky Beer Brats, each brat cut in half (giving you 8 chunky pieces)
2 cups homemade French Onion Soup or 1 can Wolfgang Puck French Onion Soup and ½ can of water or stock
¼ cup red wine
2 tablespoons unsalted butter
2 tablespoons flour
Sea salt and freshly ground black pepper

1. Put a liner in the slow cooker. Make several layers of potatoes, sprinkling Mrs. Dash on each layer.

2. Add the carrots and the halved brats.

3. Mix the French onion soup and red wine, and pour it over everything in the slow cooker. If you are using the canned soup, also add ½ can of water or stock.

4. Let cook for 8–10 hours on simmer. If the potatoes don't seem fully cooked, elevate temperature to high for 30 minutes. If you have made this with your own homemade leftover French Onion Soup, you can omit the butter, flour, salt and pepper and serve it at this point. My recipe for French Onion Soup produces a thick, luxurious soup that will cook down into the potatoes and brats and will not need any extra thickening. However, if you are making this with canned soup, which is generally much thinner than homemade, proceed to step 5.

5. Take all the potatoes, brats, and carrots out and put them in an ovenproof serving dish. Keep them warm in a 200°F oven.

6. Melt the unsalted butter in a small sauce pan, and add the flour. Stir to incorporate and make a roux.[31] Cook on low for a couple of minutes, but do not brown the flour.

7. Add the still-warm cooking liquid to the roux from the slow cooker, ladle by ladle, stirring constantly to thicken the sauce.

8. Carefully adjust salt and pepper, and pour the sauce over the potatoes, brats, and carrots.

Serves 4

---

31 A roux is the basis for many classic sauces. A roux thickens your sauce and is made by simply cooking equal amounts of flour and butter for a few minutes over low heat to eliminate any raw flour taste. The roux is now ready for you to add a warmed liquid to it—in this case, the onion soup.

SOUTHERN NEW YEAR'S DAY GOOD-LUCK DINNER: HOPPIN' JOHN FOR A FAMILY

Hoppin' John is a traditional Charleston dish that is now served all through the South. Although I'm a Northerner by birth, this is the dish I serve every year on New Year's Day. I usually invite a lot of friends over and cook up a big mess of Hoppin' John, collards, brown rice, and corn bread. Pecan pie and banana puddin' are my staples for dessert. Everyone drinks lots of red wine and shares some good laughs over the past year. Please note that I always use fresh black-eyed peas, which are always available in the South in late December. If you live in another area of the country, you will probably need to use dried black-eyed peas. Make them as I describe in the first step of the recipe. Whatever you do, please don't use canned black-eyed peas because that will ruin this wonderful dish. Serve with plenty of brown rice, collards, and corn bread for a wonderful dinner to bring you good luck throughout the New Year!

2 10-ounce containers of fresh black-eyed peas or 3 cups of dried black-eyed peas
3–4 cloves garlic
2 bay leaves
1 tablespoon sea salt (only if you are using fresh black eyed-peas)
2 tablespoons extra virgin olive oil
1 onion, chopped
2 cloves garlic, minced
2 bay leaves
2 stalks celery, minced
1 red bell pepper, chopped
28-ounce can diced tomatoes
Sea salt and freshly ground black pepper
¼ teaspoon cloves
2 teaspoons miso
¼ cup vegetable stock
4 Tofurky Beer Brats
4–5 sprigs of fresh thyme, leaves removed
4–5 sprigs of fresh parsley, finely minced
Cooked brown rice

1. In a pot with a cover, cook the fresh black-eyed peas, whole garlic cloves, and bay leaves in boiling water, salted with 1 tablespoon of sea salt, for 50–60 minutes until tender. If you are using dried black-eyed peas, you need to first soak them overnight. Drain and rinse well. Put the soaked black-eyed peas, garlic cloves, and bay leaves in a large pot or Dutch oven

with just enough water to cover. Do not add salt to the water if you are cooking dried beans. Cook for at least 2 hours until tender, and then add a little sea salt to taste.

2. While the black-eyed peas are cooking, heat a large skillet. Add the olive oil, and sauté the onion until translucent. Follow with the garlic, bay leaves, celery, and red bell pepper. After about 10 minutes, add the tomatoes, salt, pepper, cloves, miso, and stock. Continue cooking for about 5–10 more minutes. Put everything except the black-eyed peas in a lined slow cooker.

3. Cook on high for about 2 hours. Add the black-eyed peas and continue cooking for another hour.

4. Sauté the brats in a lightly oiled pan. Let cool to make them easier to slice.

5. About 30 minutes before serving, slice the brats lengthwise, and then into ½-inch slices. Add the brat pieces to the slow cooker mixture. Add the thyme leaves and parsley, and adjust for seasoning. Serve over brown rice.

Serves 8–10

SOUTHERN NEW YEAR'S DAY GOOD-LUCK DINNER: HOPPIN' JOHN – FOR A CROWD

Word has gotten out about my New Year's Day Good-Luck dinners. On January 1, 2012, we had over seventy-five people join us for our traditional Southern start to the New Year. To handle a crowd of this size, I first made an enormous batch of fresh black-eyed peas (eight containers, ten ounces each). Then, I prepared two different bases – one a bit spicy and one mild. I've also included my recipe for Southern Corn Bread, as well as Nancy's Collards for a Crowd because most of my guests (including born and raised Carolina natives) told me that they were the best collards they had ever eaten.

We also had a couple of slow cookers of mac and cheese, two large wooden bowls of salad, baked ziti, six appetizers, and a sideboard groaning with a double batch of banana puddin', mocha pecan pie, brownie cheesecake pie, and homemade cookies, pecan pies, and other deserts brought by my wonderful friends. You never saw food disappear so fast! I heard several people say, "I never thought I would eat meat in Nancy's house," proving once again that if you can smile and simply say "thank you," you really can fool a carnivore.

Black-Eyed Peas

8 (10-ounce) containers of fresh black-eyed peas
10–12 cloves garlic
Water to cover
2 tablespoons sea salt

Rinse the fresh black-eyed peas in a colander. Put them in a large pot with the garlic, water to cover them, and sea salt. Cover and cook for 50-60 minutes. Don't believe the package which will say they cook in 20 minutes!

Spicy Hoppin' John

¼ cup extra virgin olive oil
2 large Vidalia onions (or other sweet onion), chopped
8 cloves garlic, minced or pressed
4 bay leaves
8 –10 sprigs fresh thyme
4 stalks celery, minced
1 red bell pepper, chopped
1 green bell pepper, chopped
28-ounce can fire roasted diced tomatoes
1 cup chopped fresh tomatoes

Sea salt and freshly ground black pepper
1 teaspoon ground cloves
2 tablespoons Worcestershire sauce, optional
2 teaspoons Texas Pete or Tabasco
1–2 teaspoons hot pepper flakes
2 14-ounce packages Tofurky Kielbasa sausages (8 sausages)
½ cup vegetable broth or stock
2 tablespoons red miso
4–5 stems of fresh parsley, chopped

1. In a large skillet, heat the olive oil and sauté the onion about 10 minutes over low heat, until translucent. Add the garlic, bay leaves, thyme, celery, red bell pepper, and green bell pepper, and continue to sauté. After about 10 minutes, add the tomatoes, Worcestershire sauce, Texas Pete or Tabasco, salt, pepper and cloves. Continue cooking over moderate heat for about 30 more minutes and then put everything in a lined slow cooker.

2. Cover and cook on high for about 2–3 hours. Turn down to low, add half of the black-eyed peas you made and continue cooking for another hour.

3. Sauté a package of Kielbasa in a lightly oiled pan. Add a little broth or stock and cook until the liquid has evaporated. Let cool.

4. About 40 minutes before serving, cut the kielbasa into small pieces (quartered lengthwise, and then chopped), and add to the slow cooker. About 10 minutes before serving, take out the thyme sprigs (the leaves will have fallen off) and the bay leaves. Add the miso and parsley, and adjust for seasoning.

Serves 35-40

Mild Hoppin' John

My mild base needs a bit of an introduction and an acknowledgment to Edna Lewis, the renowned chef from Middleton Place[32] whose food I first ate in 1988 during a memorable trip to Charleston. Edna Lewis passed away in 2006 at the age of eighty-nine. She is the author of one of my well-loved cookbooks, *In Pursuit of Flavor*. Her meatless version of Hoppin' John[33] was the first I learned to make and is the inspiration for my "mild version" of the dish.

3 tablespoons extra virgin olive oil
2 cups chopped Vidalia onion

---

32   Middleton Place is one of the most beautiful plantations on the Ashley River, just outside of Charleston, South Carolina. If you are lucky enough to find yourself in the Charleston area, please set aside a few hours to tour its lovely gardens and well-preserved buildings.
33   Edna Lewis, *In Pursuit of Flavor* (New York: Alfred A. Knopf, 1988), 50-52.

2 cloves garlic, minced or pressed
2 bay leaves
6-8 sprigs fresh thyme
4 stalks celery, minced
28-ounce can diced tomatoes
Sea salt and freshly ground black pepper
2 14-ounce packages Tofurky Beer Brats (8 sausages)
4–5 stems of fresh parsley, chopped

1. Heat a large skillet and add the olive oil. Sauté the onion about 10 minutes over low heat until translucent. Add the garlic, bay leaves, thyme, and celery and cook for 10 more minutes. Add the tomatoes, salt, and pepper and continue cooking for 30 more minutes.

2. Put a liner in your slow cooker and add the contents of your skillet to the slow cooker. Cook on high for about 2–3 hours. Turn the setting to low and add half of the black-eyed peas you made earlier and continue cooking for another hour.

3. Sauté a package of brats in a lightly oiled skillet. Let cool.

4. About an hour before serving, cut the brats into small pieces (quartered lengthwise and then chopped), and add to the slow cooker. About 10 minutes before serving, take out the thyme stems (the leaves will have fallen off) and the bay leaves. Add the parsley, and adjust for seasoning.

Serves 35–40

Nancy's Collards For a Crowd

If you can find baby collards, they are ideal for this recipe and worth the extra cost. They are very tender and easy to clean, because you don't need to remove the stem or the rib that runs down each leaf. You can just wash them thoroughly and chop them into rough pieces with a chef's knife. Baby collards also cook much more quickly than the huge collard leaves you normally find. However, if large mature collards are all you can find, don't despair. The collards will still be delicious, but will take more time to prepare and will need an extra hour or two to cook. If you are working with large collard leaves, you need to follow three steps: wash the collards thoroughly; remove the tough rib; and finely chop the leaves into quarter-inch ribbons. Here's the method I use: I cut the base of the collards where they all come together in a bunch and then I wash the leaves thoroughly. Next, I hold each leaf by the stem with my left hand, and then use my paring knife to cut down each side of the tough rib to quickly freely the green leaves on both sides of the rib. When I've done about eight leaves, I put them on the cutting board and using a chef's knife, slice them crossways into thin ribbons. Ten to twelve pounds of collards is about fifteen to twenty bunches, depending on the size of the collards, so the prep work for a large crowd will take you at least an hour unless you have help.

¼ cup extra virgin olive oil
3 large sweet onions, finely chopped
12–15 cloves garlic, pressed or minced
10–12 pounds collards (cleaned and prepared as described in the head note)
Vegetable stock, broth or water, as needed
Sea salt
Freshly ground black pepper
Crushed red pepper
Vinegar or lemon juice

1. Heat 2 very large pots over low heat and put half of the olive oil in each pot. Divide the chopped onions between the 2 pots and sauté the onions slowly over low heat until the onions are soft and translucent. This will take you about 10–12 minutes. Add garlic to each pot and cook for 2–3 minutes more—be very careful not to burn the garlic.

2. Add the collards gradually, and stir with a wooden spoon. The reason you need to start with two pots is because you will have a huge volume of collards. However, collards cook down so this enormous amount is going to diminish dramatically. I usually try to start with just the water that is still clinging to the greens from washing, but inevitably add several cups of liquid (vegetable stock, broth, or water) to each pot to keep the greens from sticking. The greens will go from very bright green to a deep, dark green in about 20–25 minutes.

3. At this point, you have a couple of choices. If you want to baby-sit the greens and keep checking the pots regularly to see if they need some liquid, you can cover and check them every 10 minutes or so. Since I need to move on to the next dish if I'm feeding a crowd, when the contents of both pans has diminished, I combine them in a lined slow cooker, set on low, and let them simmer for about 8 hours. I usually make my collards the day before the party, because they taste even better once they have had a chance to sit overnight.

4. Season with sea salt, freshly ground black pepper, a little crushed red pepper, and vinegar or lemon juice.

Serves 70–80

SOUTHERN CORN BREAD

This recipe makes one large pan of corn bread, which will serve about twelve to eighteen people, depending on how big you cut the pieces. If you need to make more to feed a crowd, just double or triple the recipe as appropriate. Our family loves corn bread, and this one is simple to make with a delicious, tender crumb. I've adapted this from Crescent Dragonwagon's addictive Dairy Hollow House Skillet-Sizzled Buttermilk Cornbread Recipe[34] – but I don't use a skillet, buttermilk or anywhere near as much butter as she does!

2 cups stone-ground cornmeal
2 cups unbleached all-purpose white flour[35]
2 tablespoons baking powder
½ teaspoon baking soda
½ teaspoon salt
¼ cup brown sugar
2 cups plain yogurt
½ cup water
2 large eggs
½ cup canola oil
2-3 tablespoons unsalted butter

1. Preheat oven to 400°F. Mix the cornmeal, flour, baking powder, baking soda, salt, and brown sugar in a large mixing bowl.

2. In a small bowl, mix the yogurt, water, eggs, and oil. Mix the wet ingredients into the dry ingredients with just a few strokes. Don't over mix or your corn bread will not have a tender crumb.

3. Melt the butter and pour it into a 11 x 13-inch baking pan that has been greased with butter[36] or sprayed with cooking spray. Pour the corn bread mixture into the prepared pan and bake for 30–35 minutes. Let cool slightly before serving.

Serves 12–18

---

34 Crescent Dragonwagon, *Passionate Vegetarian*, (New York: Workman Publishing, 2002), 451–452.
35 I use King Arthur Unbleached All-Purpose White Flour.
36 Put a pat of butter on a folded paper towel and grease the bottom and sides of your baking pan.

CASSOULET

This classic French recipe normally calls for lamb, goose, and sausages. How could I concoct a dish that made Julia Child swoon without using all that meat? I found that the key is to use several meat analogues. I think the combination of Tofurky Kielbasa, Tofurky Italian Sausage, WestSoy Seitan, and MorningStar Farms Veggie Bacon Strips (or Lightlife Smart Bacon) provides a lot of meaty flavor without compromising my vegetarian principles.

2 cups dry organic navy beans
1 onion, peeled but left whole
3 sprigs parsley
2 bay leaves
4 cloves garlic, peeled but left whole
Sea salt
3 tablespoons olive oil (divided use)
1 large onion, chopped
3–4 cloves garlic, pressed or minced
2 stalks celery, minced
½ cup carrots, diced
¾–1 cup dry white wine
2 bay leaves
3-4 sprigs of thyme
4 tablespoons tomato paste
½ cup vegetable broth or stock
1 cup diced tomatoes
Sea salt and freshly ground black pepper
8-ounce package WestSoy Seitan Strips, cut into small bite-sized pieces
4 Tofurky Kielbasa sausages (14-ounce package)
2 Tofurky Italian sausages (half of the 14-ounce package)
6 strips MorningStar Farms Veggie Bacon Strips or Lightlife Smart Bacon
1½ to 2 cups slightly stale Italian or French bread
¼–½ cup minced fresh Italian parsley
1 tablespoon unsalted butter

1. Put the beans in a large pot, bring to boil and boil uncovered for 2–3 minutes. Cover and let stand for one hour. Drain off the water, and put the beans in the pressure cooker, along with another two quarts of water, and the whole onion, parsley, bay leaves, and whole garlic cloves. Cook for about 5 minutes, and then turn off the heat. Let the pressure go down naturally (it will take at least 20–30 minutes). When the pressure is off, carefully remove the

lid, taste the beans to make sure they are tender enough and if they are, add a little sea salt to taste. If they are not tender enough, put the lid to the pressure cooker back on, and cook for another 5 minutes. If you don't have a pressure cooker, just put the soaked beans, whole onion, garlic, and herbs in a large soup pot with a lid and simmer for about an hour or two. Taste the beans and make sure they are tender enough, and if not, cook them longer. Once the beans are tender enough for you, use a slotted spoon to take out the whole onion, garlic, and herbs. Add a little sea salt if the beans need it.

2. Preheat oven to 400°F. Coat a deep 2.5–3-quart casserole dish with a little olive oil or non-stick cooking spray.

3. Heat 2 tablespoons olive oil in a skillet, and sauté the remaining chopped onion for 7-8 minutes over low heat, until translucent. Add the garlic, celery, and carrots, and sauté for at least 5 minutes more. Add wine, bay leaves, thyme, tomato paste, tomatoes, and seitan. Cook for 10–12 minutes, adding stock if necessary.

4. In a small skillet, sauté the bacon strips. Drain on paper towels. Cut or crumble the bacon strips into small pieces and add to the tomato/onion mixture simmering in the larger skillet.

5. Sauté the sausages in 1 tablespoon olive oil until lightly browned. Let cool on paper towels. When cool enough to handle, cut into ½-inch pieces.

6. Using a slotted spoon, ladle about one-third of the warm beans into the casserole dish. Add a layer of half of the tomato/onion mixture, followed by half of the sausage pieces. Repeat, ending with a layer of beans.

7. Buzz the bread in the food processor to make crumbs. Mix in the parsley. Spread the bread and parsley mixture over the top layer of beans. Dot with tiny pieces of unsalted butter.

8. Bake uncovered for 50–60 minutes until nicely browned. Let rest for about 5-10 minutes before serving.

Serves 8

Sweet and Sour Cabbage with Kielbasa

Since my father was Hungarian and I grew up in Cleveland, I enjoy making many delicious dishes from Hungary, Poland, Russia, Austria, and other eastern European countries. The trouble is that most of them are very meat-centric! Here's my new slow cooker take on an old classic. This is a flexible dish that can be made in as little as three hours, or five or more hours if you're at work. I've filmed a video of how to make this dish, so please watch it at http://www.ehow. com/ehow-food.

2 tablespoons extra virgin olive oil
1 medium red onion, chopped
1 medium red cabbage, cored, very thinly sliced, and finely chopped.
4-5 carrots, peeled and cut into 2-inch matchsticks
1 large Granny Smith apple, peeled and grated
Sea salt and freshly ground black pepper
1 teaspoon caraway seeds
¼ cup apple cider vinegar
1 tablespoon cornstarch
¼ cup white wine or vermouth
½ cup stock
¼ cup brown sugar
4 Tofurky Kielbasa (14-ounce package), each sausage cut in half

1. Heat the oil in a small saucepan and sauté the onion for about 4–5 minutes. Add the red cabbage and carrots and cook for 8 minutes. Add the grated apple, and stir in the vinegar to keep the apple from browning. Season with sea salt, freshly ground black pepper, and caraway seeds.

2. Put a liner in your slow cooker and add the contents of your skillet.

3. In a small bowl, whisk the cornstarch, wine, stock, and brown sugar. Season with a little more sea salt and pepper and pour it over the cabbage mixture. Cover and cook on low for 3 hours or high for 2 hours.

4. Bury the kielbasa in the cabbage, and cook on low for about 2 more hours or on high for an hour if you're in a hurry to eat.

5. Adjust seasonings and serve with potatoes rosti or mashed potatoes.

Serves 4

POLISH KIELBASA WITH SAUERKRAUT

If you are on a low-sodium diet, don't make this dish because sauerkraut has a ton of sodium. Please try my next kielbasa recipe with cabbage instead. I use sauerkraut in a jar rather than canned sauerkraut because it tastes so much better. There are many fine brands, but I prefer Gundelsheim Barrel Sauerkraut from Germany—no preservatives, just cabbage and salt. Serve this hearty dish with a good seeded rye bread.

850-milliliter jar of sauerkraut
1 tablespoon canola oil
1 tablespoon unsalted butter
1 small onion, finely minced
4 Tofurky Kielbasa (14-ounce package)
16 new red or white potatoes, scrubbed but not peeled
1 teaspoon caraway seeds
1 teaspoon dill weed
Freshly ground black pepper
½ cup vegetable stock
½ cup white wine

1. Put liner in the slow cooker and add the sauerkraut.

2. Melt the butter and oil, and sauté onion for about 5–6 minutes. Put the onions on top of the sauerkraut and then bury the potatoes and Kielbasa in the sauerkraut. Sprinkle with caraway seeds, dill, and freshly ground black pepper.

3. Add the stock and white wine.

4. Cook on high at least 4 hours or 6 hours on simmer. Add more stock, if needed.

Serves 4

CLASSIC KIELBASA (WITH CABBAGE, POTATOES, AND MUSHROOMS)

Growing up in Cleveland in the 1960s and 1970s, there were many ethnic enclaves in the inner city. One was called Slavic Village. The restaurants in that neighborhood served an interesting mix of Polish, Slovenia, Slovak, Croatian, and Russian cooking. I had a wonderful Polish boyfriend for many years, so I became accustomed to the tastes (and smells) associated with that style of ethnic cooking. A recent visit to Cleveland proved that Slavic Village is nothing like the ethnic enclave near where I grew up. However, when I made this in the slow cooker, it brought back a lot of interesting memories. We served it with a well-chilled dry Riesling.

¾ cup boiling water
4 ounces dried shiitake mushrooms
¼ cup plus 2 tablespoons dry white wine (divided use)
1 onion, thinly sliced
1 tablespoon canola oil
1 tablespoon unsalted butter
8-10 white button mushrooms, cleaned with a mushroom brush or paper towel and sliced
1 small head of green or red cabbage, cored and very thinly sliced
12-16 red or white new potatoes, scrubbed, but not peeled, and cut in half
14-ounce package Tofurky Kielbasa, sliced into 1-inch chunks
¼-½ cup vegetable stock or broth – only if needed
Sea salt and freshly ground black pepper

1. Pour boiling water over the shiitake mushrooms. Add 2 tablespoons white wine and let sit for about 15 minutes. Remove the mushrooms from the soaking liquid, saving the liquid for later in the recipe. Remove and discard the mushroom stems, and thinly slice the caps.

2. While the shiitake mushrooms are softening, heat a large skillet and sauté onion in unsalted butter and oil. Add the sliced button mushrooms to the onion, followed by the shiitake mushrooms once they are softened.

3. Put liner in slow cooker. Put the sliced cabbage in the bottom of your slow cooker.

4. Put the potatoes on top of the cabbage, followed by the sliced Kielbasa, and then the onion-mushroom sauté.

5. Top with mushroom soaking liquid and the remaining ¼ cup white wine, along with a little salt and a lot of pepper.

6. As your dinner cooks, check the slow cooker occasionally to make sure that the liquid hasn't evaporated. If more liquid is needed, add a little stock or broth.

7. Cook for at least 6 hours on high, adding more stock, broth or water if needed. Serve with rye bread or crusty rolls and my Polish Cucumber Salad.

Serves 4

POLISH CUCUMBER SALAD

Most of the versions of this salad remove the seeds, heavily salt the cukes, and let them sit. I don't like salty, watery cucumbers, so my version is very different and more suitable for folks who need to be careful about their sodium intake. I don't use large cucumbers for this salad – I like the small Kirby cukes, which are about 4–6 inches long. I think this salad is a refreshing counterpoint to the Kielbasa, which can be a bit heavy.

4 Kirby cucumbers, peeled, halved lengthwise, seeds removed, and sliced
Sea salt
⅓–½ cup low-fat sour cream
½ large lemon, juiced
1-2 tablespoons finely minced fresh dill weed
Freshly ground black pepper

1. Place the peeled, halved, and sliced cukes in a bowl. Sprinkle lightly with salt and let sit about 10 minutes. Drain any juice that accumulates.

2. Add the sour cream and lemon juice. Mix lightly.

3. Sprinkle with dill weed and add lots of freshly ground black pepper.

4. Chill for about 15 minutes before serving.

Serves 4

Autumn in Eastern Europe

The hearty, Eastern European style of cooking can be "different" to our American palates. I think it provides a wonderful way to eat with the seasons. Cabbage is abundant year round, but it's never better than in the fall. Find a local farmer who grows cabbage without pesticides. Even if it is not labeled organic, you will be in for a healthy, delicious, and inexpensive treat. I paired the cabbage with golden delicious apples cooked with apple cider in my slow cooker, Field Roast Smoked Apple Sage Sausage, and kasha (cooked buckwheat groats). If you can't find Field Roast in your stores, a package of Tofurky Kielbasa will also work well.

1 medium head of green or red cabbage, thinly sliced
1 sweet onion, chopped finely
3 apples, peeled and chopped
1–1 ½ cups of fresh apple cider
¼ cup brown sugar
3 tablespoons apple cider vinegar
Sea salt and freshly ground black pepper to taste
2–3 tablespoons fresh dill weed, finely chopped (optional)
1 teaspoon caraway seeds
1 package Field Roast Smoked Apple Sage Sausage
1 cup buckwheat groats
1 large egg, lightly beaten

1. Mix all of the ingredients (except the sausage, buckwheat groats, and egg) in a lined slow cooker. Cook for 6-8 hours on low.

2. Grill 1 package of Field Roast Smoked Apple Sage Sausage, after first extricating them from their casings. Grill marks look great, but don't overcook. You need to be careful because these sausages can be fragile. Add the grilled sausages to the cabbage-apple mixture in the slow cooker while you make the kasha.

3. Make the kasha by stirring together the buckwheat groats and egg in a cast-iron skillet, sprayed with cooking spray. After about 3–4 minutes, add 2 cups boiling water. Cover the pan and cook for 15 minutes over low heat. After 15 minutes, add a little sea salt to taste and stir. Turn off the heat and leave covered for another 3–5 minutes.

4. Put a sausage on each plate, along with a healthy amount of the cabbage-apple mixture and the kasha. If you eat dairy, this dish is also good with a dollop of sour cream.

Serves 4

Potato, Kale, and Sausage Gratin

Inspired by Deborah Madison's "humble" creation (her words, not mine) from *The Savory Way*,[37] I wanted to jazz up the concept, and create something of my own. Donnie, a local farmer at the Charlotte Regional Farmers' Market, had beautiful baby kale one Saturday. The price was right (two bags for $5), so I experimented with kale recipes all week. The kale leaves are so small and tender that preparation is ridiculously easy, with no need to cut the kale leaves from the stems. I don't recommend using regular kale for this recipe. Deborah's delicious version alternates layers of russet or yellow Finnish potatoes and kale under a blanket of rich cream. I wanted to add more protein, so I incorporated Field Roast Smoked Apple Sage Sausage. The sausage is made with Yukon gold potatoes, apples and rubbed sage, but it is delicate and needs to be handled with care. I also sprinkled the top of this dish with fresh goat cheese and panko. Thank you for the inspiration, Deborah and Donnie! Serve with a Pinot Noir.

1 teaspoon salt
1 pound russet potatoes, peeled and sliced into ¼-inch thick rounds
2 Field Roast Smoked Apple Sage Sausages (half the package)
6–8 ounces baby kale, washed well and sliced into very thin ribbons
Unsalted butter or canola oil
Sea salt and freshly ground black pepper
1¼ cups cream
4 ounces fresh goat cheese
2–3 tablespoons panko

1. Bring a large pot to boil about half-filled with water, and add the salt. Put the sliced potatoes in a deep steamer insert and submerge them in the boiling water. Cover the pot and let the potatoes cook for about 10–12 minutes. The potatoes should yield slightly when pierced with a knife, but won't be fully cooked.

2. Preheat the oven to 350°F. While the oven is heating, remove the casing on the sausages, and grill them for a few minutes over medium heat until just barely starting to color. If you don't have a grill handy, a lightly oiled skillet will work. Let the sausages cool slightly. Split them lengthwise and cut into ½-inch pieces or just save time and crumble them with your hands.

3. Take the steamer insert out of the boiling water and put the potatoes in a colander to cool. Put the steamer insert back in the pot, along with the sliced ribbons of baby kale. Cook for 5–6 minutes, and then put the baby kale in a separate colander to drain and cool. You

---

37   Deborah Madison, *The Savory Way* (New York: Bantam Books, 1990), 223.

should have about 2 cups of bright green cooked baby kale. Don't throw away that beautiful, healthy cooking liquid. Put it in clean mason jars and make some delicious soup tomorrow.

4. Lightly oil or butter a gratin dish, and then layer the kale, potato, and sausage in alternating bands. Sprinkle each band with a little sea salt and freshly ground black pepper. Pour the cream over the top. Sprinkle with crumbled goat cheese and panko. Cover tightly with non-stick foil and cook for 30–35 minutes. Remove the foil and cook for another 15–20 minutes until the potatoes are fully cooked and the liquid is completely absorbed.

Serves 4

ASPARAGUS RISOTTO WITH APPLE SAGE SAUSAGE

I have become so enamored with the Field Roast Smoked Apple Sage Sausage that I am constantly looking for new ways to use it. I thought that it gave a fresh and very different flavor to my favorite asparagus risotto recipe. We enjoyed this with a bottle of D'Orsoria Pinot Grigio and the company of good friends.

1 pound asparagus, bottoms snapped off and reserved, tips left whole, and stalks cut into 1-inch pieces
4–5 cups vegetable broth or stock
2 tablespoons unsalted butter
1 onion, finely chopped
1 cup diced red or orange bell pepper
1½ cups uncooked Arborio rice
¼ cup dry white wine
⅛ teaspoon freshly ground black pepper
1 tablespoon extra virgin olive oil
2 Field Roast Smoked Apple Sage Sausages (half of the package), casings removed, sausages quartered lengthwise, and chopped into small pieces
¾ cup grated Parmigiano-Reggiano cheese (plus extra for the table)
Sea salt and freshly ground black pepper

1. Prepare your asparagus. Heat the broth or stock in a medium sauce pan over low heat. I add the bottoms of the asparagus stalks to the broth or stock to give it a richer taste. Just cook them for about 10-12 minutes while your vegetables are sautéing, and then discard the bottoms of the stalks or add to your compost pile.

2. Heat a large skillet and melt the butter. Add onion and sauté for 5–6 minutes. Add bell pepper pieces to the onion and sauté for at least 3 more minutes. Add the rice, and sauté for a minute or two before adding the wine. Sauté until the wine is completely absorbed, about 2–3 minutes. When the rice has completely absorbed the wine, add the asparagus and then begin adding warm broth or stock, about ½ cup at a time. Cook and stir until liquid is absorbed. Keep adding liquid until the rice is just barely al dente.

3. Meanwhile, heat olive oil in a medium skillet, and cook the sausage pieces for about 3 minutes until lightly browned.

4. When the rice is al dente, add the sausage pieces, turn the heat very low, and cover for another minute or two. Stir in cheese and a little sea salt and pepper to taste. Turn off the heat. Cover and let stand for a minute. Stir again, adjust the seasonings and serve immediately.

Serves 4–5

FOOL A CARNIVORE

...WHO LOVES BEEF!

BEEF AND MUSHROOM STROGANOFF

Beef analogues are tricky. Even if the texture is good, it's going to be very hard to replicate the meaty taste of beef. That's why a killer sauce is key. The sauce will take you about twenty-five to thirty minutes, but be patient, because it is worth the time and effort. The beefless tips or steak strips will take only three to five minutes to cook, so you can still have dinner on the table in less than forty minutes. Serve with buttered noodles, sprinkled with the optional poppy seeds. I love to combine everything rather than serving the noodles separately—your choice! I've filmed a video of how to make this dish, so please watch it at http://www.ehow.com/ehow-food.

2 tablespoons unsalted butter (plus an additional 2 tablespoons if serving the noodles separately)
½ cup chopped red onion
3–4 shallots, minced
3 cloves garlic, pressed
2 cups sliced mushrooms
5–6 sprigs of thyme, leaves removed
1 bay leaf
2 tablespoons cognac (optional)
1 tablespoon cornstarch
½ cup vegetable stock or broth
¼ cup red wine
1–2 teaspoons Dijon mustard
1 teaspoon Worcestershire sauce[38]
Sea salt and freshly ground black pepper
9-ounce package Gardein Home Style Beefless Tips or 6-ounce package Lightlife Smart Strips Steak Style Strips
1–1½ cups sour cream
2–3 tablespoons chopped parsley
1-pound package wide egg noodles
Poppy seeds (optional)

1. Melt butter in a large skillet. Sauté red onion for 4–5 minutes over medium heat. Add shallots and cook from another 2–3 minutes. Add the garlic last and cook a minute or two more.

2. Lower the heat slightly. Add mushrooms, thyme, and bay leaf and cook slowly for about 10 minutes over medium-low heat.

---

38   Most commercially prepared Worcestershire sauce contains anchovies. If that bothers you, either omit the Worcestershire sauce, or use a vegan version. We've tried several and think that Annie's Natural Organic Worcestershire Sauce tastes closest to the real thing.

3. Add cognac and sauté gently until the cognac is gone. Whisk the cornstarch into the stock. Add the red wine, and then part of the stock to the onion/mushroom mixture. The sauce will begin to thicken nicely. Add mustard, Worcestershire sauce, sea salt, and pepper to your simmering sauce.

4. Keep adding small amounts of stock or wine until the sauce is medium thick (it should be thick enough to coat the back of a spoon). Taste your sauce carefully and adjust seasonings.

5. Add the beefless tips or steak strips to the sauce and let cook for 3–5 minutes. Stir in the sour cream and heat gently. Add the parsley and adjust seasonings.

Serves 4

Pot Roast

Seitan is a good stand-in for beef, if you are craving those Sunday beef brisket dinners of your youth. I recommend WestSoy Cubed Seitan, in the blue box. If you decide to use another brand of seitan, make sure that you choose one that is not designed for stir-fries, since they are usually heavily seasoned with tamari. This is an incredibly easy dish to make in the slow cooker and only needs about ten to fifteen minutes of time to make the sauce when you come home.

16-20 small new potatoes, either white or red
1 pound carrots, cut in 2-inch pieces
12 pearl onions
4 cloves garlic, left whole
2 bay leaves
5 sprigs of thyme
3–4 sprigs of Italian parsley
2 8-ounce boxes WestSoy Cubed Seitan, sliced into ¼-inch slices
2 stalks of celery, cut on the diagonal in 1-inch slices
2 garlic cloves, pressed
¾ cup red wine, plus more as needed
2 cups vegetable stock, plus more as needed
Sea salt and freshly ground black pepper
2 tablespoons unsalted butter
2 tablespoons unbleached all-purpose flour
1 teaspoon red or brown rice miso
1 teaspoon brown sugar

1. Put a liner in the slow cooker, and then add in order, potatoes, carrots, onions, garlic, bay leaves, thyme, and parsley.

2. Add the seitan, and any juice from the package over the top of the veggies. Add the celery, which will cook the quickest, then the pour the red wine and stock and sprinkle with salt and pepper.

3. Set the slow cooker to simmer for 6 hours, but check it after 4 hours. If too much liquid has evaporated, add more stock and/or more red wine.

4. At around 6 hours, preheat oven to 200°F so that you can keep everything warm while you make your sauce. Put the veggies and seitan in a lightly oiled baking dish and cover with foil while you prepare the gravy. Put the baking dish in the oven. Put the remaining liquid into a glass measuring cup so you can gauge how much liquid you have from the slow cooker.

5. Melt unsalted butter in a small sauce pan. Add flour and make a roux.[39] Add the reserved liquid from the slow cooker, and additional liquid (either stock or wine) until you have at least a cup of liquid. Add the miso and brown sugar, and stir until completely dissolved. Continue cooking over a low heat, tasting every few minutes. Add more wine, stock, or seasonings to taste.

6. Remove the baking dish from the oven and pour the sauce over the veggies and seitan.

Serves 4–6

---

39   A roux is the basis for many classic sauces. A roux thickens your sauce and is made by simply cooking equal amounts of flour and butter for a few minutes over low heat to eliminate any raw flour taste. The roux is now ready for you to add a warmed liquid to it—in this case, the liquid from the slow cooker.

Beef and Mushrooms Berkeley

I've made many versions of Anna Thomas's venerable Mushrooms Berkeley from the 1972 classic *The Vegetarian Epicure*.[40] The idea of cooking down all that red wine into a rich sauce, with the mushrooms and peppers becoming "very dark and evil looking" was tantalizing to me as a young cook. Enter Deborah Madison's Mushrooms Flagstaff, from *The Savory Way*.[41] Deborah wisely reduced the brown sugar, used dried shiitake mushrooms as a base, and added some tofu for more protein. Over the years, I've made numerous variations of both recipes. This is my latest version which uses the Gardein Home Style Beefless Tips. We serve it with a full-bodied Cabernet Sauvignon.

3 tablespoons unsalted butter
1 onion, diced
1 green bell pepper, cut in ½-inch squares
1 red or yellow bell pepper, cut in ½-inch squares
8-12 ounces crimini or baby portobello mushrooms, wiped clean with a paper towel and halved
1¼ cups dry red wine
¼ cup brown sugar
2 tablespoons Dijon mustard
2 tablespoons Worcestershire sauce[42]
Sea salt and freshly ground black pepper
2 9-ounce packages Gardein Home Style Beefless Tips
6.5-ounce packet Kashi 7 whole grain pilaf, made according to package directions, or 1 cup brown rice, steamed for 50-55 minutes

1. Melt the butter in a large skillet, and add the diced onion. Sauté for 5–6 minutes until translucent and softened, and then add the peppers. Cook for 3 minutes, and then add the mushrooms. Cook uncovered over low heat for at least 8 more minutes.

2. While the vegetables are cooking, mix the red wine, brown sugar, mustard, Worcestershire sauce, lots of freshly ground black pepper, and a tiny bit of sea salt, and pour the mixture over the simmering onions, mushrooms and peppers. Let the sauce simmer for about 15 minutes.

3. When the sauce is reduced, add the beefless tips, and cook for another 5–6 minutes. Adjust seasonings and serve over Kashi 7 whole grain pilaf or brown rice.

Serves 4–6

---

40   Anna Thomas, *The Vegetarian Epicure* (New York: Vintage Books, 1972), 140.
41   Deborah Madison, *The Savory Way* (New York: Bantam Books, 1990), 128-129.
42   Most commercially prepared Worcestershire sauce contains anchovies. If that bothers you, either omit the Worcestershire sauce, or use a vegan version. We've tried several and think that Annie's Natural Organic Worcestershire Sauce tastes closest to the real thing.

FRENCH ONION SOUP

This is the only main dish recipe in my book that doesn't contain a meat analogue. That's because homemade French onion soup is such a special treat and tastes so meaty that I wanted to share my recipe with you. I have served this to many carnivores and have never been asked if I made it with beef stock. I get my beefy taste from a vegan bouillon cube called Not-Beef, which I sparingly use (because of its high sodium content) to deepen the flavor of the vegetable stock. This is a time-consuming preparation, but for me, there is no more rewarding way to spend a chilly winter weekend afternoon than making this delectable soup for my family. I learned to make this soup from Julia Child during one of her French Chef cooking shows when I was in my early teens, and have often consulted her very different versions in *The French Chef Cookbook*[43] and *Julia Child & More Company*[44] for inspiration. If you have some soup left over, please use it to make my French Onion Brats.

4 tablespoons unsalted butter (divided use)
2 tablespoon extra virgin olive oil (divided use)
5–6 large onions, very thinly sliced (about 6 cups)
1 teaspoon sea salt
¾ teaspoon sugar
3 tablespoons unbleached all-purpose flour
6 cups vegetable stock
2 cups water
1 Not-Beef bouillon cube
1 cup red wine
3 bay leaves
3 sage leaves
3–4 sprigs thyme
3–4 sprigs parsley
3 tablespoons cognac (optional)
Freshly ground black pepper
Baguette or a good quality loaf of French bread
4–5 ounces Gruyere cheese, grated
1 cup grated Parmigiano-Reggiano

---

43   Julia Child, *The French Chef Cookbook* (New York: Alfred A. Knopf, 1968), 275-277.
44   Julia Child, *Julia Child & More Company* (New York: Alfred A. Knopf, 1979), 108-118.

1. Heat a large, deep-sided skillet, and add 3 tablespoons of the butter and 1 tablespoon of the olive oil. Add the thinly sliced onions and stir to coat them with the melted butter and oil. Cover and cook over very low heat for about 20–25 minutes until the onions are translucent and very tender. Lift the lid every 5 minutes or so and give them a stir. They should reduce in volume slightly and give off an incredibly succulent aroma.

2. Uncover the skillet and turn the heat up a few notches. Add the sea salt and sugar, both of which will help the onions caramelize. Cook for another 30 minutes or so, stirring frequently, until the onions are a lovely golden brown and greatly reduced in volume.

3. Reduce the heat again, add the remaining tablespoon butter, and stir the flour into the nicely browned onions. Cook for a minute or two. While you're doing this, heat your stock and add the water and bouillon cube. You should have a total of 8 cups of liquid.

4. Add the liquid gradually and stir well to make sure the flour doesn't lump. Add the wine, bay leaves, sage, thyme, parsley, and freshly ground black pepper. Let the soup simmer for about 30 minutes or so. Remove the bay leaves, sage, thyme, parsley, and adjust seasonings.

5. Preheat the oven to 350°F. Slice the baguette into ½-inch thick slices. Put the slices on a lightly greased baking sheet, and brush the slices lightly with the remaining tablespoon of olive oil. Bake them for about 15 minutes or so, until they are golden. Remove from the oven and let them cool on a wire rack. Julia says that these are called *croûtes* (similar to an overgrown crouton, but actually more like an Italian crostini in appearance).

6. Lightly grease individual ramekins or ovenproof soup bowls with a little olive oil or butter. Put them on another baking sheet. Grate your cheeses and combine them.

7. Put 1 or 2 of the *croûtes* in the bottom of the individual ramekins or bowls so that they cover the bottom. Sprinkle with cheese, and then ladle in a little of the delicious soup. Add another layer of croûtes, more cheese and more soup. End with a layer of croûtes and cheese at the top of the bowl. Put them in the oven for about 20 minutes until the cheese is bubbling. Remove them from the oven and let them cool for a few minutes. The soup will be scalding hot, so don't burn yourself.

Serves 4–6

FOOL A CARNIVORE

. . .WHO LOVES CHICKEN!

CHICKEN PICCATA

I've recently discovered Gardein Lightly Seasoned Chick'n Scallopini in the freezer section of my local supermarket. They are low in calories (110 calories per two-and-a-half-ounce cutlet) and each cutlet has fourteen grams of protein. I use finely chopped Baby Vidalia onions (they look like scallions on steroids), which are easy for me to find in the farmers' markets in early spring. If you can't find them, I suggest substituting four or five shallots, finely minced. The flavor will be a bit different, but the dish will be just as good. This is a very simple dish to prepare and can be on your table in less than fifteen minutes. We enjoy it with garlic mashed potatoes, steamed snow peas, and a light Pinot Grigio. I've filmed a video of how to make this dish, so please watch it at http://www.ehow.com/ehow-food.

10-ounce package of Gardein Lightly Seasoned Chick'n Scallopini
3–4 tablespoons unbleached all-purpose white flour
Sea salt and freshly ground black pepper
4 tablespoons extra virgin olive oil (divided use)
2 small Baby Vidalia onions, finely chopped or 4–5 shallots, finely minced
½ cup white wine
3–4 tablespoons capers, rinsed and drained
1 large lemon, zested and juiced
2 tablespoons unsalted butter
2–3 tablespoons Italian parsley, chopped

1. Keep the Gardein Lightly Seasoned Chick'n Scallopini frozen until you're ready to cook them. Put the flour in a shallow bowl, and season it with a little sea salt and pepper. Dredge the frozen cutlets in the seasoned flour.

2. Heat 2 tablespoons olive oil in a large skillet. Sauté the Chick'n Scallopini for 2–3 minutes on each side. Remove from the skillet and set aside on a plate while you make the sauce.

3. Sauté the onions (or shallots) in 2 tablespoons olive oil for 5–6 minutes. When translucent, add the white wine to deglaze the pan and cook over low heat until the volume is reduced by half.

4. Turn the heat very low. Add the capers, lemon zest, lemon juice, and butter. Whisk or stir the sauce to make sure that everything is well incorporated. Cook for 3–4 minutes. Taste and correct seasonings. Return the Chick'n Scallopini back to the pan to lightly reheat, turning once to coat both sides with the sauce. Garnish with the fresh chopped parsley.

Serves 4

Pesto Chicken

Our son, Nick, told me that I need to create more chicken recipes. So, while he was home for Thanksgiving break from Stetson University, I thought about how to include pesto in a recipe without doing my traditional pesto Genovese with pasta, green beans, and potatoes. I decided to use Quorn Naked Chik'n Cutlets to give Nick a pesto fix without pasta. I served it with steamed green beans, garlic roasted potatoes, and some crusty bread. I can also suggest sautéed zucchini and yellow squash with lemon and buttered orzo pesto as two other great accompaniments to this dish.

1 package Quorn Naked Chik'n Cutlets (4 cutlets)
3–4 ounces pesto (preferably homemade – my pesto recipe follows)
1 cup pasta sauce (home or store bought)
¼ pound fresh mozzarella
¼ cup pine nuts

1. Remove the package of Quorn Naked Chik'n Cutlets from the freezer and let them thaw for about 30 minutes. Make your fresh pesto while the Cutlets are thawing. If you are using homemade frozen pesto (see my recipe below), take it out of the freezer and let it thaw in a small bowl of very warm water.

2. Preheat the oven to 400°F. Lightly spray the bottom and sides of a baking dish with cooking spray, and then spread the pasta sauce.

3. Place the slightly thawed cutlets on the pasta sauce (rounded side up), and then spread pesto on top of the cutlets.

4. Grate or slice the mozzarella and sprinkle over the layer of pesto. Top with pine nuts. Bake for 20 minutes.

Serves 4

MY FAVORITE PESTO

Since we are blessed with a long growing season in the Carolinas, I grow my own basil from mid-April through early October. I usually buy at least six to eight basil plants and grow them organically. We reap an incredible amount of basil and enjoy pesto often. In fact, it is our son's most requested "comfort food." I freeze pesto in four-ounce jars, which are the perfect size for one recipe. I love dipping into my freezer in January and pulling out a tiny green jar that reminds me of summer.

One note: I am a very flexible pesto maker, and don't always use the same proportions. Pesto is a very forgiving sauce, and as long as all your ingredients are fresh and delicious, it really won't matter if you use a little more or less of certain ingredients. Make sure you always use only the basil leaves—never the stems or the tops that have begun to flower. The flowering tops will make your pesto taste nasty!

3 cups fresh basil leaves
3–4 garlic cloves, pressed
½ cup pine nuts, lightly toasted
Sea salt
About 2/3 cup extra virgin olive oil
½ cup freshly grated Parmigiano-Reggiano cheese
3–4 tablespoons freshly grated Pecorino Romano cheese
2 tablespoons unsalted butter, softened (optional)

1. Put the basil leaves, garlic, pine nuts, and a tiny bit of sea salt into the food processor. Turn it on and begin drizzling in the olive oil, blending well. Scrap the sides of the food processor.

2. Taste and adjust the salt (but use a very light hand, because you're still going to be adding cheese). If you are making this batch to freeze, never add cheese at this point. You'll freeze it without cheese and add cheese when you thaw it out for your pasta.

3. Assuming you're eating it tonight, stir in the grated cheeses and use the pesto for the pesto chicken recipe. But if you've made the pesto for pasta, here's what you should do: before you drain your pasta, reserve a cup of the pasta water. Drain the pasta in a colander and put it back in the hot pot. Add the pesto, toss well with a couple tablespoons of unsalted butter. Then add the cheeses. Toss again and add a little of the pasta cooking water to thin the pesto slightly so that it will coat the pasta like silk. Serve with additional grated Parmigiano-Reggiano cheese.

LEMON ROSEMARY CHICKEN

This is my take on a tried-and-true classic Italian combination. With only 110 calories and seventeen grams of protein per cutlet, you should add this tasty recipe to your repertoire of easy weeknight meals. I prepare the cutlets in a variety of ways—and my son keeps telling me that I need to invent more. This is a very simple recipe because the marinade can be prepared in the morning before you leave for work. The cutlets sit all day in the fridge, soaking up the delicious marinade. We especially like the Lightlife Smart Cutlets because of their texture and grill marks. We enjoyed this dish with spinach risotto that was left over from another dinner, and steamed green beans. Pair this dish with a well-chilled Soave or Pinot Grigio.

4 Lightlife Smart Cutlets Original (2 packages)
3 lemons, squeezed (about ¼ cup of juice)
Lemon zest from 2 of the lemons
4–5 cloves garlic, left whole
4 fresh rosemary sprigs
3–4 parsley sprigs
3–4 thyme sprigs
¼ cup extra virgin olive oil
2 tablespoons white wine
1–2 tablespoons Worcestershire sauce[45]
1½ tablespoons Dijon mustard
Mrs. Dash Lemon Pepper Seasoning
Sea salt and freshly ground black pepper

1. Unwrap the cutlets and put them in a container that has a lid. Mix all of the other ingredients in a bowl and then pour the marinade over the cutlets. Poke holes in the cutlets with a fork so that the marinade will seep in. Cover, and let the cutlets marinate in the refrigerator for about 8 hours.

2. Grill for about 2 minutes on each side. Be careful not to overcook them!

Serves 4

---

45   Most commercially prepared Worcestershire sauce contains anchovies. If that bothers you, either omit the Worcestershire sauce, or use a vegan version. We've tried several and think that Annie's Natural Organic Worcestershire Sauce tastes closest to the real thing.

Ravioli Mornay with Chicken, Cauliflower, and Spinach

I learned to make a mean béchamel sauce from watching Julia Child on *The French Chef*. I remember my mom making something she called "white sauce" with chipped beef and green peas over mashed potatoes. Although it was emphatically not my favorite meal, I was intrigued with the process of how to make a sauce. Julia, bless her, taught me how very simple it is to make a delicious basic sauce.

First, heat a medium sauce pan and melt butter—then add an equal amount of flour.[46] Stir for a minute or so over low heat to thoroughly incorporate the flour. Voilà—you've just made a roux. Cook the roux for a minute or two over low heat to eliminate any raw flour taste. Then gradually add warm liquid, stirring until you have a beautiful rich sauce. If you use milk as your liquid, it's a béchamel. Substitute stock for milk and you have a velouté. Add a mixture of grated Gruyere and Parmesan to the béchamel, and you have a Mornay sauce. You have just learned how to make three classic French sauces in a few minutes!

I used cauliflower as one of my two vegetables because its pale color makes it literally disappear into the Mornay sauce. Baby spinach is the second vegetable and doesn't even need to be cooked. All you have to do is wash it well, cut it in narrow ribbons, and put it in the bottom of the colander before you dump in the pasta water and ravioli. The boiling pasta water will cook the ribbons of baby spinach in a few seconds. Lastly, my technique of cooking the Quorn Chik'n Tenders is something I haven't seen before. The package advises you to sauté them in oil on the stove top for twelve minutes. I shorten the cooking time and jazz up the flavor by dousing them with some white wine delivered in two doses. They cook thoroughly in about eight minutes with this method, and we thought they tasted even better than the way we had previously prepared them. We enjoyed this dish with a buttery Chardonnay sitting out on our deck on a warm March evening.

2½ cups milk
2 cups cauliflower, broken into florets
2 cups baby spinach, sliced into thin ribbons
2 tablespoons unsalted butter
½ cup finely minced shallots
2 tablespoons flour
Few dashes nutmeg
Sea salt and freshly ground black pepper
½ cup grated Gruyere cheese

---

46   The proportions of butter and flour to your liquid determine if your sauce is thin, medium or thick.

¼ cup grated Parmigiano-Reggiano cheese
1 tablespoon extra virgin olive oil
12-ounce package Quorn Chik'n Tenders
½ cup dry white wine (divided use)
13-ounce package mini cheese ravioli
2–3 tablespoons cream or milk

1. Warm the milk in a small sauce pan. Do not let it boil.

2. Fill a large pasta pot with water. Cover the pan and let it come to a boil over high heat. Steam the cauliflower in a steamer for about 10 minutes. Put the spinach ribbons in a colander in your sink.

3. While the cauliflower is steaming, melt the butter in another sauce pan and sauté the shallots for 4 minutes. Add the flour and cook for another minute or two to make a roux. Gradually add the warm milk, stirring frequently, until it is completely incorporated. Stir in a bit of nutmeg, salt, and pepper. Turn the heat down and let the sauce continue to cook until it is thick enough to coat the back of a spoon. Add both cheeses, stir to incorporate well, and then cover and take the sauce pan off the heat.

4. Heat a skillet over medium heat. Add the olive oil, and when the oil has heated, add the Quorn Chik'n Tenders. After about 4 minutes of sautéing, douse them with ¼ cup of white wine. About 2 minutes later, repeat with the remaining ¼ cup of white wine. Cook until the wine is almost gone, with less than a tablespoon or so of liquid remaining in the pan. Taste one of the tenders to make sure it is thoroughly cooked. It should be delicious. Turn off the heat and cover the skillet.

5. Add a tablespoon or two of salt to the boiling water and put in the mini ravioli. They will float to the top when they are done, which should be in about 5–6 minutes.

6. Uncover your Mornay sauce, put it back over low heat and give it a few stirs. It should be pretty thick. I usually add a couple of tablespoons of cream (or milk) to slightly thin it. However, you still want it to be a fairly thick sauce because there will be a little moisture with the Chik'n Tenders and the cauliflower and spinach that will thin it out.

7. Remove the pasta pot from the stovetop and pour the cooked ravioli and all the boiling pasta water over the spinach ribbons that have been patiently waiting in the bottom of your colander. The jolt of boiling water should cook the thin spinach ribbons perfectly. Return the ravioli and the spinach to the still hot pasta pot. Add the cauliflower, Chik'n Tenders, and the Mornay sauce. Stir well. Taste carefully and correct seasoning.

Serves 4

CHICKEN CACCIATORE (WITH A TWIST)

Since *cacciatore* literally means "hunter," the vegetarian cook should hunt for the very best fresh mushrooms available. Make sure your mushrooms smell fresh and earthy, with firm, dry stems and unblemished caps. This dish is lovely with a variety of mushrooms, but it will be good even if you can only find the familiar white button mushrooms from your local grocery store. Always wipe the mushrooms clean with a dry paper towel or a soft mushroom brush – never wash them with water. I deepen the sauce's mushroom flavor by using Pacific Organics Mushroom Stock and the good red wine we intend to drink with the meal. Most chicken cacciatore recipes ask you to brown the chicken first, and then use the pan drippings to build your sauce. Here, I construct the sauce first, and then add the meat analogue directly to the sauce. I originally developed this dish with Delight Soy Nuggets from my local Earth Fare. I recently revisited the recipe using Quorn Chik'n Tenders, and was pleased with the results. We usually enjoy this dish with a Chianti Classico.

12 ounces Delight Soy Nuggets (see head note) or 12-ounce package of Quorn Chik'n Tenders
2 tablespoons extra virgin olive oil
½ cup minced onion
2 stalks celery, halved lengthwise and thinly sliced
12 ounces baby portobello, crimini, or other type of mushrooms, sliced
2 cloves garlic, minced or pressed
28-ounce can diced tomatoes
2 bay leaves
2–3 sprigs of fresh rosemary
½ teaspoon of hot red pepper flakes
½ cup red wine
1½ cups vegetable stock or mushroom stock (see head note)
Sea salt and freshly ground black pepper
2–3 ounces Manchego cheese, grated
2–4 tablespoons freshly grated Parmigiano-Reggiano

1. If you are using the Delight Soy Nuggets, you may have purchased them refrigerated or frozen. Please thaw them if they are frozen. If you are using the Quorn Chik'n Tenders, take them out of the freezer and let them start thawing while you make the sauce.

2. Heat a large skillet and add the olive oil. Sauté the minced onions over low heat for 5–6 minutes. When the onions are translucent, add the celery and mushrooms and sauté for 8–10 minutes. Add the garlic and sauté for another minute.

3. Add the tomatoes, hot pepper, rosemary, bay leaves, salt, and pepper. Let the sauce cook for about 8–10 minutes with the lid off, stirring occasionally.

4. Add wine, stock or broth, as needed as your sauce simmers and reduces. Cook for at least 10–15 minutes.

5. Add the nuggets or tenders to the simmering sauce and turn the heat down a bit. Cook about 3 minutes if you are using the Delight Soy Nuggets or about 10 minutes if you are using the Quorn Chik'n Tenders.

6. Turn the heat to low. Sprinkle on the Manchego cheese and Parmigiano-Reggiano and put the lid on the skillet. Let it cook gently for about 3 minutes until your cheese is completely melted.

Serves 4–6

Chicken Pomodoro

In this recipe, I made a bow to traditional chicken recipes by cooking the cutlets first. However, unlike real chicken, the analogue cutlets cook in just two to three minutes on each side. Take the cutlets off the heat and let them rest on a plate while you make the simple, delicious sauce, which is a variation of a vodka pasta sauce that my family dearly loves. I serve this dish with buttered pasta and broccoli or green beans topped with freshly grated Parmigiano-Reggiano. We paired it recently with an outstanding 2009 Masseria Cavallo Negroamaro from Puglia, but a good Sangiovese or Zinfandel would also match it nicely.

2 tablespoons extra virgin olive oil
4 Lightlife Smart Cutlets Original (2 packages) or 12-ounce package of Gardein Lightly Seasoned Chick'n Scallopini
2–3 cloves garlic, minced or pressed
3 tablespoons vodka
28-ounce can fire roasted crushed tomatoes
½ cup diced tomatoes
½–1 teaspoon of red pepper flakes
Sea salt and freshly ground black pepper
3–4 tablespoons cream cheese
2–3 sprigs of fresh basil or Italian parsley, finely minced

1. Heat the skillet and add the olive oil. Sauté the cutlets for 2 minutes on each side, and then set aside.

2. In the same skillet, sauté the garlic for a minute or so. Add the vodka and cook for 2–3 minutes to deglaze the pan.[47]

3. Add the crushed tomatoes, diced tomatoes, red pepper flakes, salt and pepper, and cook for 10–12 minutes until your sauce has slightly reduced and thickened. Use the time while the sauce is cooking to prepare your veggies or make a salad and set the table.

4. Add the cream cheese, and let simmer on very low heat for 2–3 minutes. Add the minced basil or parsley. Return the cutlets to the creamy tomato sauce and gently reheat.

Serves 4

---

47 "Deglaze" is just a fancy cooking term for adding some liquid (usually wine or stock) to a pan in which you've already cooked something, and then heating that liquid to help loosen any cooked bits of food that may be lurking on the bottom or sides of the pan. Although deglazing is usually done after you cook meat in a pan to help form the foundation of a sauce, there are still some bits of food that remain from cooking the meat analogues, so I've adapted the technique to my style of cooking.

Coq au Vin

One of the difficulties of adapting traditional French recipes is the sequence in which you add ingredients. Most French cookbooks ask you to sauté the chicken pieces first, in order to make sure that they cook for the required length of time and really build the flavor of the sauce. Many vegetarian chicken analogues can change in texture if they cook too long, which is why I reorder the method of cooking to add them later in most cases. The recipe sequence is adapted for our son Nick, who hates mushrooms, but you can sauté the mushrooms in the same pan after sautéing the onions, shallots and garlic if no one in your family has a similar pathological hatred! (I actually prefer to do it this way if our son is not around.) The second difficulty in making Coq au Vin is that the dish is traditionally made with large pieces of chicken, like legs, wings and thighs, whose look would be impossible to duplicate with a chicken analogue product. Here I've used either the Quorn Chik'n Tenders or the Delight Soy Nuggets. The Quorn Chik'n Tenders will be much smaller and more uniform in size, so you need to pretend that you cut up the chicken into small pieces. If you use the Delight Soy Nuggets, which are pounded flat and are rather irregular in size, they actually look like small pieces of chicken breast. My husband and I prefer this recipe with the Delight Soy Nuggets, because we enjoy their chewy texture. Serve with asparagus, new potatoes with parsley and chives or buttered egg noodles, and the same wine you used in cooking–preferably, a lovely Côtes du Rhône, Pinot Noir, or Burgundy.

4–5 tablespoons unsalted butter (divided use)
½ pound baby portobella, crimini, or white mushrooms (halved or quartered, depending on their size)
Mrs. Dash Garlic and Herb Blend
Sea salt and freshly ground black pepper
1 tablespoon extra virgin olive oil
1 small onion, minced
4–6 shallots, minced
2 cloves garlic, minced or pressed
2 tablespoons bleached all-purpose flour
1¼–1½ cups dry red wine (divided use)
1¼–1½ cups vegetable stock or broth (divided use)
1–2 tablespoons cognac, optional
2 bay leaves
4–6 sprigs fresh thyme
6–8 MorningStar Farms Veggie Bacon Strips
1 tablespoon tomato paste (or 1 tablespoon finely chopped sun dried tomatoes)
1 package Quorn Chik'n Tenders or 1 pound Delight Soy Nuggets

1. Heat a large deep sauce pan and melt 2 tablespoons butter. Sauté the mushrooms for 7–8 minutes, adding a few shakes of Mrs. Dash Garlic and Herb, as well as sea salt and pepper. Set the mushrooms aside.

2. Add 1 tablespoon butter and 1 tablespoon olive oil to the sauce pan in which you cooked the mushrooms and sauté the minced onions for 7–8 minutes over low heat, followed by the shallots for 3–4 minutes, and then the garlic for a minute.

3. In the same sauce pan, add 1-2 tablespoons unsalted butter (depending on how much butter is still in the pan). Stir in the flour and cook for about 2 minutes, but don't let the flour brown. You are making a roux.[48]

4. Add 1 cup of red wine, 1 cup of stock, cognac, bay leaves, and thyme. Stir fairly frequently, so that your sauce doesn't form lumps.

5. Spray a skillet with cooking spray, heat it over moderate heat, and add the frozen bacon strips. Cook for about 4 minutes on each side until crisp. Watch them carefully, because they can easily burn in the last minute of cooking. Remove from the skillet and let the bacon strips rest on a double thickness of paper towels until cool. When they are cooled, crumble them into small pieces.

6. While making the bacon strips, continue cooking the sauce. Add the tomato paste, bay leaves, thyme sprigs, salt and pepper and cook for another 5–6 minutes. Add a little more wine and stock as the sauce reduces and thickens. The sauce should be thick enough to coat the back of a spoon. If the sauce seems too thick, thin it with a little stock. If the sauce seems too thin, cook it a bit longer. Remove the bay leaves and thyme sprigs. Taste carefully and correct seasoning.

7. Add the crumbled bacon and chicken analogue. If you are using the Quorn product, cook about 8 minutes. If you are using the Delight Soy product, it will cook in about 4 minutes. Let everything simmer gently for another 2–3 minutes to combine flavors.

Serves 4

---

48   A roux is the basis for many classic sauces. A roux thickens your sauce and is made by simply cooking equal amounts of flour and butter for a few minutes over low heat to eliminate any raw flour taste. The roux is now ready for you to add a warmed liquid to it—in this case, a mixture of wine and stock.

GUMBO

This recipe could have just as easily gone under the sausage category, but since I had fewer chicken recipes, guess where it landed? To make a great Gumbo, you need to have an interesting combination of flavors, meats, and textures. Some folks make this more as a soup, but we like it as a stew with brown rice. As a consequence, my gumbo recipe will be a bit thicker and more substantial than others you might try.

I've recently revised this recipe to use Field Roast Mexican Chipotle sausage, instead of the Tofurky Kielbasa that I'd previously used. Both are very good, but the Field Roast really gives it a spicy flavor that my dear Cajun husband confided was missing in the previous incarnation of this dish. If you eat seafood, I suggest adding a pound of peeled, deveined shrimp when you add the sausage. It will really round out the flavor and will make your carnivores very, very happy.

A word or two about okra is in order. A lot of people think that they hate okra, or only like it fried. Their aversion to okra may be because they think it is slimy. If you've had slimy okra, it's because it hasn't been properly prepared. Never let okra touch water. You should wipe okra with a dry paper towel, in the same way as you clean mushrooms. Washing okra with water at the prep stage is a recipe for disaster. Choose the very smallest okra pods you can find, cut off the caps and tips and slice them into quarter-inch rounds. They will cook in the gumbo in about ten to twelve minutes, and will thicken the sauce nicely.

There are actually three ways to thicken gumbo, and I use two of the three ways in this recipe. The three ways are to use a brown roux, okra, or gumbo filé powder (made of dried sassafras leaves). Technically, you only need one to thicken the gumbo. However, we love okra, along with the dark, deep taste of a properly prepared brown roux, so I decided to use both in this dish. A brown roux is different from the roux you've made in several of my other recipes. A brown roux needs to cook for a <u>long</u> time—at least forty-five to sixty minutes. Before you gasp at that amount of time, please keep in mind that if your sauce pan of roux is slowly cooking next to your big pot of gumbo, it will be an easy task to stir the roux from time to time as it slowly browns. The roux needs to cook to at least a medium brown color before you add it to the gumbo. Given the proportions of this recipe, you're only going to add half of the roux you make. I know you're wondering why on earth you would make twice the amount of roux you need for a recipe. Here's my answer. A well-made brown roux is so time consuming that it doesn't make sense to make a tiny amount. You can easily refrigerate the balance for about a week or two, until you have a craving for gumbo again or want to make another Cajun recipe, like jambalaya. Trust me – once you make a recipe with a proper brown roux, you will see so much depth of flavor that you will be looking for other Cajun dishes to make.

On another note—I've seen a lot of strange wine pairings with gumbo suggested online (a Sauvignon Blanc or a Riesling . . . really?) We enjoyed our delicious gumbo with a 2004 Castle Rock Pinot Noir.

½ cup canola oil

½ cup unbleached all-purpose white flour

2 cups raw brown rice

2 tablespoons extra virgin olive oil

2 cups finely chopped onion

2–3 stalks celery, sliced in half lengthwise and then chopped into ¼-inch slices, about 1 cup

3 cloves garlic, minced or pressed

1 green or red bell pepper, chopped into ½-inch squares, about 1½ cups

2 tablespoons Worcestershire sauce, optional

⅛ teaspoon allspice

⅛ teaspoon ground cloves

1 cup vegetable stock and up to an additional ½ cup if needed

1 cup crushed tomatoes

28-ounce can diced tomatoes

2 bay leaves

4–6 sprigs of thyme

2 cups sliced okra (prepared as described in the head note)

2 Field Roast Mexican Chipotle Sausage or 2 Tofurky Kielbasa, sliced lengthwise in quarters and then sliced in ¼-inch pieces

12-ounce package Quorn Chik'n Tenders or 2 7-ounce packages of Gardein Chick'n Strips

2 tablespoons finely minced parsley

Sea salt and pepper

Brown rice

1. Begin making the roux in a small, heavy-bottomed sauce pan. Heat the canola oil, and then add the flour with a whisk. Turn the heat very low, and stir occasionally as it begins to turn darker in color. This will take about 45–60 minutes. You do not have to stir it constantly, but you do have to be aware of how it is progressing and not let it burn.

2. After you get your brown roux started, begin cooking your brown rice. Rinse the brown rice well. Either steam it in a rice steamer according to your steamer's directions or and put it in a medium sauce pan along with 3 cups boiling water or broth, along with a little sea salt and cook covered over low heat for about 45-50 minutes. Taste the rice, fluff with a fork, and keep covered until you're ready to serve.

3. While the rice and the roux are cooking, heat a large skillet. Add the olive oil and sauté onion for about 5–6 minutes until it begins to soften. Add the celery and sauté about 4 minutes, and then add the garlic and cook for another minute or two.

4. Add the green or red bell pepper pieces and sauté for 4–5 minutes. Add the Worcestershire sauce, bay leaves, thyme, allspice, cloves, 1 cup stock, crushed tomatoes, and diced tomatoes. I just put in the whole bay leaves and thyme sprigs, and remember to remove them before serving.

5. Stir well, cover, and cook over moderately low heat for another 10 minutes. Add the okra and cook for 10 minutes more.

6. Stir in the chicken tenders or strips, cover and cook for 8 minutes.

7. Depending on the thickness of the sauce at this point. You may need to add up to ½ cup of stock in order to thin it enough to add about half of the roux that you've been faithfully cooking. I know what you must be thinking, "If the sauce is already thick enough, why do I need to add the stupid roux you've asked me to cook?" The reason is that the gumbo just won't have the same flavor without the brown roux. So, add a little more of the stock and then add about half the lovely brown roux you've been tending.

8. Uncover the skillet, add the minced parsley, and cook for about 5 more minutes. Taste carefully and adjust seasonings with salt, pepper and any of the spices you've used. Mound some brown rice in the center of a soup bowl and ladle the gumbo around it. If you're not counting carbs, soak up every last bit with a crusty baguette.

Serves 6–8

PENNE WITH ASPARAGUS, GOAT CHEESE, AND CHICKEN

Quorn Chik'n Tenders are usually my go-to product for any dishes I create that involve cut-up chicken pieces. They taste good and have an excellent texture. Recently, I've noticed that the pieces are a little smaller, which is a change I like. It helps the tenders integrate better into a dish and doesn't make them as readily identifiable as a chicken analogue. You can find the Quorn Chik'n Tenders in the frozen food section of your grocery store. If you can't find them, I've also had good success using two of the Quorn Naked Chik'n Cutlets, thawed and sliced into strips. You can probably substitute other "chicken products" but I don't guarantee the same results. If your time is limited, I've had good success using a cup of roasted red peppers from a jar in this recipe. You can generally find them near the olives in your grocery store. I just rinse them off, slice them up, and add them to the sauté, which saves about four minutes of time. I've specified Baby Vidalia onions in this recipe because I love their sweet flavor and the rapidity with which they cook. However, feel free to substitute another variety of onion and just sauté them for a few minutes longer. We enjoyed this dish with a Sauvignon Blanc from New Zealand.

2 tablespoons extra virgin olive oil
2 Baby Vidalia onions, diced
2 cloves garlic, minced or pressed
1 red bell pepper, cut into very thin matchsticks
1 pound asparagus (leave the tips whole and slice the stalks on the diagonal into 1-inch pieces)
Sea salt and freshly ground black pepper
1 pound penne
10.6-ounce package Quorn Chik'n Tenders or 2 Quorn Naked Chik'n Cutlets
¼ cup dry white wine
½–¾ cup vegetable broth or stock
4 ounces goat cheese (preferably flavored with garlic and herbs, but plain will work, too)
½ cup walnut pieces, toasted
Pasta cooking water or up to ½ cup cream or half-and-half (see option in steps 5–6)
½ cup grated Parmigiano-Reggiano, plus more for the table

1. Heat a skillet and add the olive oil. Sauté the diced onions for 4–5 minutes over moderate heat until they begin to soften. Add the garlic and sauté for another minute or two. Add the red bell pepper and cook for 3–4 minutes, followed by the asparagus. (If you are using canned roasted red peppers, add them after the asparagus.)

2. Once the asparagus has been added, cook the veggies for 4–6 minutes. Bring the pot of pasta water to a rolling boil. Add 2 tablespoons of salt and watch it bubble up. Put the penne in the water and set your timer for 10–11 minutes.

3. Add the Quorn Chik'n Tenders or the cut-up pieces of the Quorn Naked Chik'n Cutlet to the skillet, along with the white wine. Cook for 2 minutes until most of the wine is gone and then add ½ cup of stock. Cover the skillet, turn the heat to low, and continue cooking while you check the pasta and determine if it is al dente.

4. If the penne needs a few more minutes of cooking, adjust the seasoning for your asparagus/Quorn mixture and cut up the goat cheese into small pieces. Sauté the walnut pieces in a small skillet over low heat until lightly browned and then briefly buzz them into pieces in your food processor into pieces. Grate the Parmigiano-Reggiano.

5. Reserve a cup of pasta water, before you drain your pasta into a colander. I normally just take a Pyrex cup measure and dip it into the pasta water before draining. You won't need a full cup—probably between ⅓ cup and ½ cup, but it's easiest to just do it this way. On the other hand, if you don't care about calories, you can use half-and-half or cream in place of the pasta water.

6. Put the pasta back into the pasta pot, and add the asparagus and Quorn mixture, followed by the goat cheese. The goat cheese should begin melting and get very creamy. Add some of the reserved pasta water, half-and-half, or cream to loosen the sauce, a few tablespoons at a time. Add ½ cup Parmigiano-Reggiano, and stir again.

7. Sprinkle with toasted walnut pieces and pass additional grated Parmigiano-Reggiano at the table.

Serves 6

SWEET AND SOUR CHICKEN

I originally put this under Easy Weeknight Meals until I made it again and timed myself at each step. Unless you have done all your prep work in advance (which means cutting your vegetables and preparing the sauce before you leave for work), this recipe will take forty-five to sixty minutes, which pushes it into the Weekend Dinner category. We like either the Boca Original Chik'n Nuggets or the Quorn Chik'n Nuggets in this dish. Please note that there are different cooking temperatures and times in the recipe depending on which brand of chicken analogue you use. The breading in either brand stands up well to the sauce and the nuggets have a pleasant, meatlike texture when added to the sauce at the last minute. This dish does not reheat well because microwaving the nuggets in the sauce makes them soggy, so if you make more than you can consume that night, leave some of the nuggets out of the sauce to add upon re-heating. I recently used a fresh pineapple rather than canned unsweetened pineapple chunks and it made an incredible difference in the taste. If you decide to use whole fresh pineapple, cut off the top and the bottom and stand it upright on your cutting board. Cut the skin off the sides of the pineapple in long strips with a sharp, flexible knife. If there are still some small brown eyes left from the skin, remove them with the tip of your knife or a potato peeler, just as you would with the eyes of a potato. Stand the pineapple on its base, and cut the pineapple in half and then in quarters. Lay each slice on its side and cut out the core. Cut each slice into 1-inch chunks, removing and discarding the core. Using a fresh pineapple in the dish will add an additional five to six minutes of prep time, but the resulting dish will be brimming with fresh flavor and will make you wonder why you ever used canned pineapple in any recipe.

10-ounce package Boca Original Chik'n Nuggets or 10.6-ounce package Quorn Chik'n Nuggets
1 small onion, cut in half and sliced into very thin rings
2–3 stalks celery, sliced into ¼-inch pieces on the diagonal, about ¾ cup
3 carrots, sliced into ¼-inch pieces on the diagonal, about 1 cup
1 red or green bell pepper, cut into thin matchsticks
1 large bunch broccoli, stems peeled and sliced on the diagonal, and florets separated (yielding at least 2 cups)
5–6 mushrooms, cut in half
3 baby bok choy, washed well, bottoms removed, and sliced into ½ inch pieces
5–6 scallions, thinly sliced
2 tablespoons canola oil or peanut oil
½ cup toasted cashew pieces (optional)
20-ounce can unsweetened pineapple chunks, juice reserved or 2 cups fresh pineapple, prepared as described in head note and cut into chunks (plus ½ cup pineapple juice)
2 tablespoons orange mango juice or orange juice
1 tablespoon freshly squeezed lemon juice

2 tablespoons apple cider vinegar

¼ cup brown sugar (the pre-measured ¼-cup packets by Dixie Crystals are perfect for this recipe)

2 tablespoons low sodium soy sauce or tamari

2 tablespoons umeboshi plum vinegar or rice wine vinegar

2 tablespoons San-J Orange Sauce (optional, but very good)

2 tablespoons cornstarch

Brown or white rice (depending on how much time you have)

1. Depending on which meat analogue you're using, preheat the oven to either 400°F (for Boca) or 425°F (for Quorn). Put the rice on to steam and begin preparing the vegetables while the oven preheats.

2. Assuming you've prepped your veggies in advance, oil your wok, and begin stir-frying the vegetables in the order listed. This will take you about 10–12 minutes. If you are really pressed for time, cover your wok (which I know is a heresy) for about 3–4 minutes and that will help your veggies cook more quickly.

3. Put the nuggets in the oven for 10 minutes for Boca or 15 minutes for Quorn.

4. If you are using cashews, this would be a good time to toast the cashew pieces in a small skillet over low heat. Don't let them burn.

5. Either cut your fresh pineapple in chunks (see head note) or drain the canned pineapple chunks and reserve the juice. Pour the pineapple juice in a small bowl and add all of the remaining ingredients (except for the cashews). Whisk in the cornstarch thoroughly so that there are no lumps.

6. Add the sauce to the stir-fried veggies, and stir over high heat for about 3–4 minutes until the sauce thickens. Add the pineapple chunks and cook for another minute. Stir in the nuggets, and serve over brown or white rice, with the optional toasted cashews sprinkled on top.

Serves 4

Okra and Tomatoes with Chicken

Normally I slice my fresh okra pods into neat quarter-inch rounds. However, if I can find small, tender okra at the market which are about two inches long, it is a delicious treat to use the whole pod. Clean the okra by just wiping the pods with a dry paper towel, and cutting off the little caps at the stem end of each pod. Never let water touch okra or it will be slimy. This is a quick little recipe that will satisfy a Southerner's craving for great end-of-the-season vegetables like okra, tomatoes and sweet corn because I've eliminated the steps needed to create a proper brown roux. (If you want to learn how to make a brown roux, please see my Gumbo recipe.) Couscous and buttery ears of sweet corn would be the perfect accompaniment to this dish. This is a great recipe for vegans[49] that will even fool carnivores!

1–2 tablespoons extra virgin olive oil
1 sweet onion, chopped
2–3 cloves garlic, minced or pressed
1 cup chopped yellow bell pepper
2 cups small okra pods, wiped clean and caps removed
3–4 tomatoes, chopped
¾–1 cup V8 juice (low-sodium)
3 sprigs of thyme
1 sprig of oregano
1–2 teaspoons Worcestershire sauce[50]
Sea salt and freshly ground black pepper
12 ounces Delight Soy Nuggets or 12-ounce package Quorn Chik'n Tenders, thawed
1 teaspoon gumbo filé (dried sassafras leaves), optional

1. Heat a skillet and add the olive oil. Sauté the onion for 4–5 minutes. Add the garlic, and then the yellow bell pepper. Sauté for about 5 more minutes.

2. Add the okra pods and cook for about 8–10 minutes. Add the tomatoes, and let them cook down. Then add the V8 juice, thyme, oregano, Worcestershire sauce, salt, and pepper. Taste and correct seasonings.

---

49   This will be a vegan dish if you use the Delight Soy Nuggets. It won't be vegan if you use the Quorn Chik'n Tenders, since they contain a small amount of egg white.

50   Most commercially prepared Worcestershire sauce contains anchovies. If that bothers you, either omit the Worcestershire sauce, or use a vegan version. We've tried several and think that Annie's Natural Organic Worcestershire Sauce tastes closest to the real thing.

3. Add the Delight Soy Nuggets, and let simmer for 2–3 minutes. If you are using the Quorn Chik'n Tenders, let them simmer about 8–10 minutes, because they take a little longer to cook. Just before serving, stir in the optional gumbo filé powder.

Serves 4

Baked Chicken, Okra, and Tomatoes over Pepper Jack Grits

For me, okra was a learned taste. However, after thirty years of living in the South, okra has become a vegetable that I associate with great food. I created this recipe as a way of using up a half pound of okra that didn't have a home—not really enough to fry, and surely not enough to make another recipe of gumbo. Okra is highly perishable, so if you let it stay in the fridge more than a day or two, it will start to turn brown and you'll need to exile it to the compost pile. Make sure that you take the Quorn Naked Chik'n Cutlets out of the freezer before you leave for work, and let them thaw in the fridge. Except for the time-consuming process of making real corn grits, this recipe clocks in at around thirty-five to forty minutes, which puts it a just a wee bit north of my thirty-minute meal mark. If you're willing to use instant grits as the base for the Pepper Jack Grits, and do a little prep work in advance, this can probably still qualify as an Easy Weeknight Meal. However, we love the taste and texture of the slow-stirred, stone ground yellow corn grits, so we are willing to spend that additional cooking time to make this on a weekend.

1–2 tablespoons extra virgin olive oil
2 Baby Vidalia onions, tops and roots removed, cut in half and thinly sliced
2 cloves garlic, pressed
1 medium red, yellow, or orange bell pepper, cut into thin matchsticks
¼ pound mushrooms, cleaned and sliced (about 2 cups)
½ pound small okra pods, wiped clean and sliced in thin rounds (a little less than 2 cups)
28-ounce can diced tomatoes or diced fire roasted tomatoes
4 sprigs thyme
3 sprigs oregano
2 sprigs parsley
Sea salt and freshly ground black pepper
1 package Quorn Naked Chik'n Cutlets (4 cutlets), thawed
3 sprigs parsley, finely minced

1. Preheat oven to 400°F. Heat a skillet and add the olive oil. Sauté the onions for 5–6 minutes. Add the garlic and sauté for a minute, and then the bell pepper. Cook for 3–4 minutes.

2. Add the mushrooms, and sauté for 4–5 more minutes.

3. Clean the okra (see head note) while the mushrooms are sautéing. Add the okra and sauté for about 2–3 minutes before adding the tomatoes. Put in the whole sprigs of thyme, oregano and parsley (you'll take them later). Cover and let simmer for about 15 minutes.

4. Take out the herb sprigs, taste, and correct seasoning. Make sure the okra is tender enough. If not, cover the skillet and cook it a little longer.

5. Lightly oil 4 small individual baking dishes or one small rectangular baking dish that will hold all 4 cutlets. Put a little of the sauce on the bottom and then put in the cutlets with the rounded side facing up. Pour the sauce over the cutlets. Bake for 10 minutes. Sprinkle with fresh minced parsley. Serve with Pepper Jack Grits.

Serves 4

Pepper Jack Grits

4 cups water
½ teaspoon salt
1 cup stone ground corn grits
¼ cup cream (or slightly more–up to ⅓ cup)
3–4 ounces pepper Jack cheese, grated
Freshly ground black pepper

1. Put water in a medium sauce pan, cover and bring to a boil. Uncover and add salt and then slowly stir in the grits.

2. Keep the grits at a simmer and continue stirring. It's going to take you at least 45 minutes of stirring to produce good grits, and may take as long as an hour.

3. When the grits are starting to soften enough for you, begin adding the cream, a tablespoon at a time. When the taste and texture feel smooth enough for you, add the cheese. Turn the heat off or way down. Stir for about 2 minutes until the cheese is fully incorporated into the grits. Sprinkle with lots of freshly ground black pepper and enjoy. (Since this recipe may make a bit more than you need for your dinner, have the leftover grits with an egg for breakfast the next morning and learn why so many Southerners love grits!)

Serves 4–6

ORANGE MUSTARD-GLAZED CHICKEN WITH ROASTED RED PEPPERS

I created this dish one evening when I realized that I had a tremendous number of root vegetables that needed to be eaten. A well-loved dish in Deborah Madison's *Vegetarian Cooking for Everyone* directly inspired my roasted root veggie recipe that follows this recipe.[51] The chicken preparation provides a slightly sweet counterpoint to the potential bitterness of root vegetables such as turnips and beets. My husband thought that it was a great combination. If you are not making the roasted root veggies (which will take over an hour in the oven), this could easily be re-classified as an Easy Weeknight Meal, because the chicken dish takes less than thirty minutes to prepare. I'd like to suggest a Chenin Blanc with this recipe. We'd previously enjoyed it with other white wines, but we recently sampled a Chenin Blanc from a South African vineyard named The Rustler that was absolutely lovely with this dish.

2 tablespoons unsalted butter
4 shallots, minced
1 cup orange juice
1 orange, zested, peeled, seeded, and cut into small pieces
1–2 teaspoons Dijon mustard
2 tablespoons honey
Sea salt and freshly ground black pepper
6–8 ounces roasted red peppers, sliced into small strips (about half of a 14-ounce jar)
10-ounce package Gardein Lightly Seasoned Chick'n Scallopini
1½ tablespoons extra virgin olive oil
2 tablespoons unbleached all-purpose white flour
2 tablespoons minced fresh parsley

1. Melt unsalted butter in a medium sauce pan. Sauté the shallots about 5 minutes until translucent.

2. Add the orange juice and cook over medium heat while you zest, peel, and seed the orange. Cook until the orange juice is reduced by about a third.

3. Add mustard and honey. Taste and adjust seasonings. Add the sliced roasted red peppers and the orange pieces. Continue to simmer over low heat to blend flavors.

---

51 Deborah Madison, *Vegetarian Cooking for Everyone* (New York: Broadway Books, 1997), 412.

4. Take the Chick'n Scallopini out of the freezer. Heat the olive oil in a large skillet. While the oil is heating in the skillet, put the flour and a little salt and pepper in a shallow bowl. Lightly dredge the Chick'n Scallopini in the flour. Sauté the Chick'n Scallopini for 2–3 minutes on each side.

5. Pour the orange sauce over the Chick'n Scallopini in the skillet. Cook on low for 1 minute or so. Garnish with minced parsley and serve.

Serves 4

Roasted Root Veggies

Extra virgin olive oil
3–4 large potatoes, peeled and thinly sliced
8–10 small turnips, peeled and thinly sliced
8–10 small baby beets (preferably golden), scrubbed well, tops removed and left whole
½ pound carrots, scrubbed, peeled, and cut into 1 inch pieces
10 cloves garlic, unpeeled
3–5 sprigs rosemary
3 fresh bay leaves
2-3 sprigs sage
4 sprigs thyme
Sea salt and freshly ground black pepper

1. Oil a large baking pan with a little extra virgin olive oil or non-stick cooking spray.

2. Toss all the veggies and the other ingredients together with several tablespoons of olive oil.

3. Bake for 450°F at 20–25 minutes. Bring out of the oven and toss. Lower heat to 375°F and bake for another 25–30 minutes. Remove the bay leaves and herb sprigs, taste carefully and adjust seasoning.

Serves 4–6

Post-Thanksgiving Skillet Pot Pie

Even vegetarians need to make good use of leftovers after Thanksgiving. This recipe assumes that you made a Quorn Turk'y Roast and ate about half to two-thirds of it. The balance should be sliced thinly and then cut into large matchsticks for this dish. If you don't have a leftover Quorn Turk'y Roast, this recipe can just as easily be made with Quorn Chik'n Tenders or Quorn Naked Chik'n Cutlets. If you make this at Thanksgiving, please save your cranberry sauce, mashed potatoes and mushroom gravy, because all of them have a role to play in this delicious dish. Nothing will go to waste and your carnivores will be ready to lick their plates!

2 tablespoons unsalted butter
1 small onion, finely chopped
1 stalk celery, finely chopped
2–3 carrots, finely chopped
1 garlic clove, pressed
¼ cup dry white wine
½–¾ cup stock or broth
1–2 tablespoons cornstarch
1½ cups milk
½ cup frozen peas, steamed for about 5 minutes
Sea salt and freshly grated black pepper
¼ teaspoon grated nutmeg
2 cups of thin strips cut from a Quorn Turk'y Roast (or 12-ounce package of Quorn Chik'n Tenders or 3 thawed Quorn Naked Chik'n Cutlets, thawed and sliced into thin strips)
3 cups of leftover mashed potatoes, warmed and thinned slightly with milk or half-and-half so they will spread easily
Leftover cranberry sauce
Leftover mushroom gravy

1. Preheat oven to 400°F.

2. In a large skillet with an ovenproof handle, melt the butter over moderately low heat and sauté the onions for 6–7 minutes until softened and translucent. Add the celery and carrots and sauté for 5 minutes more. Add the garlic and sauté for another minute or two.

3. Add the white wine and half the stock, turn up the heat slightly, and let it simmer uncovered for a couple of minutes.

4. Meanwhile, mix the cornstarch and milk in the blender, and then gradually add the mixture to the skillet. I like to alternate some stock and some milk until I achieve a thickness where the sauce coats the back of a spoon.

5. Add the peas, salt, pepper and nutmeg, and cook for 2 minutes.

6. Add the Quorn product you've decided to use, cook for 2 minutes, stir and correct seasoning.

7. Reheat the leftover mashed potatoes in the microwave or on the stovetop (thinning them with a little milk or half-and-half if needed to restore the proper consistency) and layer them on top of the skillet. Bake in the oven for 15 minutes.

8. Serve with the leftover cranberry sauce and reheated mushroom gravy.

Serves 4–6

FOOL A CARNIVORE

...WHO LOVES BACON!

Pasta All'Amatriciana

How can you possibly replicate a classic Italian dish that uses unsmoked Italian bacon (*guanicale*) made from dried "pork cheeks"? (Even some dyed-in-the-wool carnivores I know give an involuntary shudder when I asked them if they liked to eat pork cheeks!) I slowly simmer my finely diced onion and MorningStar Farms Veggie Bacon Strips with white wine and lots of red pepper flakes. It keeps the Bacon Strips from browning and imparts a delicious, deep flavor while keeping them tender. Roast your cherry tomatoes while you're simmering the onion and Bacon Strips, and the preparation will go fairly quickly. Bucatini is the traditional pasta used with this sauce. It is a thin pasta with a hole in the middle, and it may be hard to find. Feel free to substitute linguine or even spaghetti if you can't find bucatini. Serve with a big green salad, crusty Italian bread, and a crisp Soave.

1 pint red cherry or grape tomatoes, halved pole to pole
1 pint yellow cherry or grape tomatoes, halved pole to pole
Fresh herbs (several sprigs each of oregano, thyme, basil, and parsley)
3–4 garlic cloves, pressed
¼ teaspoon sea salt
3 tablespoons extra virgin olive oil (divided use)
1 small onion, minced
½ package of MorningStar Farms Veggie Bacon Strips, minced (about 1 cup)
Hot pepper flakes
1½ cups dry white wine
1½–2 tablespoons salt
1 pound bucatini
Freshly grated Pecorino Romano
Freshly grated Parmigiano-Reggiano

1. Preheat oven to 350°F.

2. Put the tomatoes in a bowl with the herbs, garlic, sea salt, and 1 tablespoon olive oil. (Sometimes I mince or tear the herbs, and other times I leave the herb sprigs whole, and remove them when the tomatoes are done roasting—your choice.) Spread on a baking tray lined with non-stick aluminum foil for easy clean up. Roast for 40–45 minutes.

3. While the tomatoes are roasting, heat a large skillet and add 1 tablespoon of olive oil. Sauté the onion over low heat for 7–8 minutes until softened and translucent. Add the remaining tablespoon of olive oil and the minced bacon strips, and sauté for about 4–5 minutes. Stir in the hot pepper flakes, and begin adding the wine, a few tablespoons at a time, until you've

used all the wine. Sauté until the wine is almost completely absorbed and you have no more than a couple of tablespoons of liquid left in your skillet.

4. Meanwhile, bring a large pot of water to a rolling boil. Add salt to the boiling water, and then your pasta. Stir and cook for the amount of time indicated on the package, testing a few minutes before it's supposed to be done to make sure it's al dente (never overcook your pasta).

5. Grate both cheeses while the pasta is cooking.

6. Reserve about a cup of water from the pasta pot. Drain the pasta in a colander and put it back in the still-warm pasta pot. Add the roasted tomatoes, along with all the juices and oil in the baking pan, along with the contents of the skillet. Toss well until everything is thoroughly mixed. If the sauce seems a little too thick, add some of the reserved pasta water to loosen the sauce, a few tablespoons at a time. (I generally add about ½ cup, sometimes more, sometimes less.) Add about ½ cup Romano and ½ cup Parmigiano-Reggiano and toss again. Dish it out into warmed pasta bowls, and sprinkle with more of both grated cheeses.

Serves 5–6

CRUCIFEROUS PASTA

Many people know that the cruciferous vegetables help fight cancer. The cruciferous vegetables are broccoli, cauliflower, cabbage, kale, kohlrabi, collards, and the dreaded brussels sprouts. With the possible exception of beets, brussels sprouts seem to strike fear into the hearts of many people. I love brussels sprouts, so I've made it a lifelong goal to find interesting ways to convince my recalcitrant husband and son that these tiny baby cabbages are worthy of inclusion in their diets—especially in a wintertime menu. Here's my latest concoction, which met with resounding approval from both of my guys.

1 stick unsalted butter
5 MorningStar Farms Veggie Bacon Strips
1 small onion, minced
1 red bell pepper, chopped
2 cloves garlic, minced
1 pound brussels sprouts, bottoms removed, and sprouts very thinly sliced
⅓ cup white wine
¼–⅓ cup stock or broth
Sea salt and pepper
¾ pound Brie, rind trimmed and cut into small pieces
Parmigiano-Reggiano, grated
1½–2 tablespoons salt
1 pound tagliatelle or fettuccine

1. Melt the unsalted butter over low heat. Pour it through a coffee filter into a bowl to remove the milk solids. You now have clarified butter.

2. Spray a small skillet with non-stick cooking spray, and cook the bacon strips until lightly brown. Don't let them burn. Remove the bacon strips to a plate covered by a double thickness of paper towels. When totally cool, crumble them.

3. Put the clarified butter in a large skillet. Over low heat, sauté the onion for 7–8 minutes until softened and translucent. Add the red bell pepper and sauté for 2–3 minutes more. Add the garlic and sauté for another minute. Add the brussels sprouts and sauté for 3–4 minutes. Add the wine, followed by the stock or broth. Cover tightly, turn the heat to very low and cook for about 12 minutes. Taste the brussels sprouts and make sure they are cooked thoroughly enough for your family. Turn off heat, add the brie, and cover.

4. Put your pasta on when you cover the brussels sprouts mixture so that everything cooks at the same time. Make sure your water is rapidly boiling, and you've added salt, right before adding the pasta.)

5. When the pasta is al dente, reserve a cup of the starchy pasta water. Drain the pasta in a colander and mix with the brussels sprouts mixture. Add some of the pasta water, a few tablespoons at a time, to loosen the sauce.

6. Serve topped with Parmigiano-Reggiano cheese and crumbled bacon strips.

Serves 4

Not Your Mom's Mac and Cheese

In the South, mac and cheese is considered a "vegetable" on most vegetable plates. I wanted to create a very different version that included a vegetable that wouldn't be readily detected. Cauliflower is the perfect foil to pasta and this recipe was inspired by one of Jamie Oliver's creations.[52] I've made a lot of changes to Jamie's original concept, but I think that the finished product still qualifies as delicious comfort food. What makes it unique is what I affectionately call "fakin' bacon" in the topping. To me, MorningStar Farms Veggie Bacon Strips are the key to the flavor of this dish. I also like to use the Barilla Plus Elbows, because the whole grain nature of the pasta is much more substantial than traditional white flour elbow macaroni. We also use both white cheddar and good quality Parmigiano-Reggiano in a sour cream sauce, which gives it much more tang and depth than the ubiquitous orange sauce that normally accompanies most mac and cheese dishes. Since this dish already has a lot of cheese and dairy, I served it with spinach and radicchio salad with dried cranberries and chopped toasted walnuts, which made a very refreshing counterpoint. I've called it a Weekend Dinner, because I felt rushed when I tried to make it in thirty minutes. However, if you want to try this on a weeknight and are super efficient, you can boil your cauliflower and pasta at the same time, while you are making the sauce, and probably clock in just a tad bit north of thirty minutes.

1 small head cauliflower, trimmed and cut into very small florets, about 3 cups
2 tablespoons salt (divided use)
1 pound elbow macaroni or small shells (ideally whole grain)
2 cups reduced fat sour cream
8 ounces white cheddar, shredded
1 cup grated Parmigiano-Reggiano
1 teaspoon Dijon mustard
½ teaspoon Worcestershire sauce[53]
3 tablespoons chopped Italian parsley
Sea salt and freshly ground black pepper
1–1½ cups bread crumbs, made from 2 pieces of stale Italian bread buzzed in the food processor
4 MorningStar Farms Veggie Bacon Strips, finely minced
½ cup grated Parmigiano-Reggiano
1 tablespoon unsalted butter, cut in very small pieces

---

52   Jamie Oliver, *Jamie's Food Revolution* (New York: Hyperion, 2008), 49.
53   Most commercially prepared Worcestershire sauce contains anchovies. If that bothers you, either omit the Worcestershire sauce, or use a vegan version. We've tried several and think that Annie's Natural Organic Worcestershire Sauce tastes closest to the real thing.

1. Preheat oven to 400°F.

2. Bring a large pot of water to a rolling boil and add 1 tablespoon salt. Put the cauliflower in a steamer basket, and let it cook for 7–8 minutes. Remove the steamer basket of the cauliflower, add the other tablespoon of salt, and put in the pasta. Cook for 6–7 minutes or according to directions on the pasta box.

3. Meanwhile, over a double boiler, melt the white cheddar and the Parmigiano-Reggiano cheeses, along with the sour cream. Be patient and cook over a low heat, stirring occasionally, and make sure that the sour cream doesn't separate.

4. Add the chopped parsley, Dijon mustard, Worcestershire sauce, sea salt, and pepper.

5. To make the delicious crumb crust, use a food processor to make the Italian bread into crumbs (or use an equivalent amount of prepared crumbs or panko). Add the minced bacon strips and Parmigiano-Reggiano and stir together.

6. Drain the pasta and cauliflower, and reserve a cup of the starchy pasta cooking water. Pour back in the warm pasta pot and add the sauce. Mix the pasta, sauce and cauliflower together. If the sauce needs a bit of thinning, use a couple of tablespoons of the pasta cooking water, using up to ½ cup. Pour the sauced pasta into a large, well-greased baking dish.

7. Evenly sprinkle the crumb mixture over the pasta. Bake for 16–18 minutes. Broil for an additional 2 minutes on low if the crust isn't crispy enough for you.

Serves 6

Farfalle with Savoy Cabbage

This recipe is not for folks who need to watch their cholesterol. If your cholesterol is within normal ranges, I think it is fine to occasionally indulge in something rich and decadent. If I have time, I'll buy a round of brie and patiently trim off the rind. However, when pressed for time, the Alouette Crème de Brie makes this recipe a snap to prepare. I use a mandoline to slice the Savoy cabbage into very thin slices, which allows it to cook rapidly.

1 tablespoon extra virgin olive oil
8–12 MorningStar Farms Veggie Bacon Strips, sliced in ¼-inch pieces
1 leek or fresh onion, finely chopped
2–3 cloves garlic, pressed
1 medium head of savoy cabbage, finely sliced
6–8 sprigs of thyme
½–¾ cup vegetable stock or broth
¼–½ cup white wine
5-ounce package Alouette Crème de Brie or 8-ounce wheel of Brie with the rind removed
4 tablespoons Alouette or fresh herbed goat cheese
3-4 tablespoons pine nuts, lightly toasted
1½–2 tablespoons salt
1 pound farfalle
Sea salt and freshly ground black pepper

1. Bring a large covered pot of water to a rolling boil for your pasta.

2. Heat a large skillet, and add the olive oil. Sauté the bacon strips for about 2–3 minutes over moderately low heat. Add the onions and sauté 5–6 minutes more. Add the garlic last, and sauté for just a minute or so. Do not let it brown.

3. Add the thinly sliced savoy cabbage to the skillet, along with the stock, thyme, and white wine. Cover and let it cook down until most of the liquid is absorbed, about 10 minutes. Check the savoy cabbage to make sure it is tender, and remove the sprigs of thyme.

4. Assuming your pasta water is at a rolling boil, add 1–2 tablespoons salt, and cook the farfalle according to the directions on the package. Reserve a cup of pasta water.

5. While the savoy cabbage is cooking, sauté the pine nuts in a small skillet over low heat until lightly browned. Set aside.

6. Add the cheeses to the cabbage once it is cooked down and softened. Taste carefully and correct seasoning, adding sea salt and pepper to taste.

7. When the farfalle is al dente, reserve a cup of pasta water, and drain the farfalle in a colander. Add the farfalle to the skillet and loosen the sauce with a few tablespoons of pasta water at a time if it seems too thick. Mix thoroughly, taste carefully, and adjust seasonings. If you have any leftovers, add some of the remaining pasta water to the pot before you divide it into smaller portions for the next day. You'll be glad that you thinned it with a little extra pasta water, because leftovers always condense in the fridge.

Serves 4–6

SPLIT PEA SOUP

A steaming bowl of split pea soup is an easy, soul-satisfying evening meal during the cold winter months. I wondered how I could get the distinctly ham flavor that is the hallmark of most split pea recipes in a meatless version. Here's my take on a familiar classic—with six MorningStar Farms Veggie Bacon Strips standing in for the ham. I use a mixture of green and yellow split peas because the colors look so lovely in the bowl.

1 tablespoons unsalted butter
1 tablespoon extra virgin olive oil
1 onion, finely diced or minced
2 stalks celery, minced
½ cup carrots, minced
2 whole cloves garlic
1 cup green split peas
1 cup yellow split peas
6 cups of water
1 cup vegetarian stock
2 bay leaves
4 sprigs of thyme
1 medium russet potato, peeled and minced
Sea salt and freshly ground black pepper
6 MorningStar Farms Veggie Bacon Strips, thawed and diced
A few slices of slightly stale baguette or French bread

1. Heat the oil and unsalted butter in a skillet. Add the onion and cook over moderately low heat for 7–8 minutes until the onion is softened and translucent. Add the celery and carrots, and cook for 4–5 minutes more.

2. While the onion, celery, and carrots are cooking, put a liner in your slow cooker, and add the split peas, stock, water, garlic, thyme, potato, and bay leaves.

3. Cook for 4 hours on high heat (or 6–7 hours on low heat).

4. About 30 minutes before serving, add the diced bacon strips to the slow cooker. While they are adding flavor, make the croutons and put a pan of biscuits in to bake. Slice the bread about ½-inch thick, and lightly brush with olive oil on both sides. Cut into small 1-inch cubes, and toast in a 350°F oven for about 8–10 minutes. Watch the croutons carefully, because they can easily burn.

5. Adjust the seasonings. Sprinkle croutons on each bowl, and serve with a freshly made buttermilk biscuit.

Serves 6–8

FIFTEEN BEAN SOUP

Whatever the number of beans in your mix (there are a lot of variations), this is the easiest recipe imaginable. I wanted the flavor of the beans to stand out, so I leave a lot of ingredients whole. This allows them to be easily removed after the beans have spent their allotted time in the slow cooker. The reason I do this is twofold. First, it makes for a quick and easy assembly. Second, the pure, but complex flavor of the many varieties of the beans comes through in the final puree. The result will be a delicious soup that is redolent with the smell of bacon. I asked my husband if he could honestly tell that it didn't have meat—he told me that if he didn't know I never cooked with meat, this soup would have fooled him. Please try it on a cold winter's evening with some crusty bread and a green salad.

2 cups fifteen-bean soup mix (or mix a little of this and that from what you have on hand to make 2 cups of beans)
1 large piece of kombu[54]
1 onion, whole
1 carrot, peeled, but left whole
1 stalk celery, whole
2 garlic cloves, whole
2 bay leaves
Freshly ground black pepper
½ package of MorningStar Farms Veggie Bacon Strips
2 fresh tomatoes, chopped (or 1 cup of canned diced tomatoes)
Sea salt

1. Soak the beans overnight, and drain off the water in the morning. (If you didn't do this the night before, pour boiling water over your beans and let them sit covered for at least an hour.)

2. Put a liner in the slow cooker. Rinse the beans and add them to the slow cooker, along with the kombu, onion, carrot, celery, garlic cloves, bay leaves, pepper, tomatoes and bacon strips. Cover with water to a depth of about an inch over the top. This should take you about 6–8 minutes.

---

54 Kombu is a type of dried edible seaweed. You can find it in your local health food store or on the internet. The benefits of using kombu when you cook your beans are that it speeds cooking time, softens the beans, and enhances the flavor of the soup. It is also reputed to make beans more digestible. Don't worry—if you can't find kombu, you can still make this soup!

3. Cover the slow cooker, set it on high for at least 8 hours (although more is OK, too, if you know you're going to need to work late), and walk out the door without a backwards glance.

4. Walk back in your home, 8-plus hours later, and be greeted with a wonderful smell. The bacon strips have done their magic and flavored the soup. Get a slotted spoon and remove them, along with the kombu, onion, carrot, celery, garlic, and bay leaves.

5. Remove about 2 cups of broth (just roughly judge this amount), and put the broth in another pot or in your food processor. (My suggestion is that it is better to remove too much than not enough.)

6. Puree the beans with a handheld immersion blender or use the food processor. I prefer the former because it gives me better control over the consistency of my puree.

7. Taste carefully and adjust seasoning, adding a bit more sea salt and pepper, or more reserved broth to obtain the consistency that looks and tastes right to you.

Serves 6–8

BIBLIOGRAPHY

Bonar, Ann. *The MacMillan Treasury of Herbs*. New York: MacMillan Publishing Company, 1985.

Bremness, Lesley. *RD Home Handbooks–Herbs*. Pleasantville, NY: Readers Digest Association, Inc., 1990.

Child, Julia. *The French Chef Cookbook*. New York: Alfred A. Knopf, 1968.

——. *Julia Child & More Company*. New York: Alfred A. Knopf, 1979.

——. *The Way to Cook*. New York: Alfred A. Knopf, 1994.

Cusick, Heidi Haughy. *Soul and Spice*. San Francisco: Chronicle Books, 1995.

Davis, Adele. *Let's Cook it Right*. New York: Signet Books, 1970.

——. *Let's Eat Right to Keep Fit*. New York: Signet Books, 1970.

——. *Let's Have Healthy Children*. New York: Signet Books, 1972.

Dragonwagon, Crescent. *Passionate Vegetarian*. New York: Workman Publishing, 2002.

Greene, Bert. *The Grains Cookbook*. New York: Workman Publishing, 1988.

——. *Greene on Greens*. New York: Workman Publishing, 1984.

Hazan, Giuliano. *The Classic Pasta Cookbook*. London: Dorling Kindersley, 1993.

——. *Every Night Italian*. New York: Scribner, 2000.

Hazan, Marcella. *The Classic Italian Cookbook*. New York: Alfred A. Knopf, 1980.

——. *Essentials of Classic Italian Cooking*. New York: Alfred A. Knopf, 1993.

——. *Marcella Cucina*. New York: HarperCollins Publishers, 1997.

——. *Marcella's Italian Kitchen*. New York: Alfred A. Knopf, 1993.

Katzen, Mollie. *The Enchanted Broccoli Forest*. Berkeley, CA: Ten Speed Press, 1982.

——. *Mollie Katzen's Vegetable Heaven*. New York: Hyperion, 1997.

——.*Moosewood Cookbook*. Berkeley, CA: Ten Speed Press, 1992.

——. *Still Life with Menu*. Berkeley, CA: Ten Speed Press, 1988.

Lappé, Frances Moore. *Diet for a Small Planet*. New York: Ballentine Books, 1973.

Lewis, Edna. *In Pursuit of Flavor*. New York: Alfred A. Knopf, 1988.

Madder, Joel. *Cleveland School Gardens*. Charleston, SC: Arcadia Publishing, 2010.

Madison, Deborah, with Brown, Edward Espe. *The Greens Cook Book*. Toronto. Bantam Books, 1987.

Madison, Deborah. *Local Flavors*. New York: Broadway Books, 2002.

——. *The Savory Way*. New York: Bantam Books, 1990.

——.*Vegetarian Cooking for Everyone*. New York: Broadway Books, 1997.

Moosewood Collective. *Moosewood Restaurant Cooks at Home*. New York: Simon & Schuster, 1994.

——. *Moosewood Restaurant Low Fat Favorites*. New York: Clarkson Potter Publishers, 1996.

——. *Moosewood Restaurant New Classics*. New York: Clarkson Potter Publishers, 2001.

——. *Sundays at Moosewood Restaurant*. New York: Simon & Schuster, 1990.

Oliver, Jamie. *Cook with Jamie*. New York: Hyperion, 2007.

——. *Jamie's Food Revolution*. New York: Hyperion, 2008.

——. *The Naked Chef*. New York: Hyperion, 2000.

Pépin, Jacques. *Jacques Pépin's Simple and Healthy Cooking*. Emmas, PA: Rodale Press, 1994.

Robertson, Robin. *Fresh from the Vegetarian Slow Cooker*. Boston. The Harvard Common Press, 2004.

Somerville, Annie. *Fields of Greens*. New York: Bantam Books, 1993.

Thomas, Anna. *The Vegetarian Epicure*. New York: Vintage Books, 1972.

——. *The Vegetarian Epicure Book Two*. New York: Alfred A. Knopf, 1978.

Weinzweig, Ari. *Zingerman's Guide to Good Eating*. Boston: Houghton Mifflin Company, 2003.

Wells, Patricia. *Patricia Wells' Trattoria*. New York: William Morrow and Company, Inc., 1993.

INDEX

Made in the USA
Lexington, KY
30 January 2013